The Middle Ages

The Middle Ages

A Watts Guide for Children

editor in chief
William Chester Jordan

FRANKLIN WATTS
A Division of Grolier Publishing
NEW YORK • LONDON • HONG KONG • SYDNEY
DANBURY, CONNECTICUT

Editor in Chief: William Chester Jordan, History Department,
Princeton University, Princeton, New Jersey

**Developed for Franklin Watts by Visual Education Corporation,
Princeton, New Jersey**

For Franklin Watts
Senior Editor: Douglas Hill

For Visual Education
Project Director: Jewel G. Moulthrop
Writers: Suzanne J. Murdico, Joseph Ziegler
Copyediting Supervisor: Maureen Ryan Pancza
Photo Research: Sara Matthews
Production Supervisor: William A. Murray
Cover Design: Maxson Crandall
Interior Design: Maxson Crandall
Electronic Preparation: Fiona Torphy
Electronic Production: Maxson Crandall, Lisa Evans-Skopas,
          Jessica Swenson, Isabelle Ulsh

Library of Congress Cataloging-in-Publication Data
The Middle Ages : a Watts guide for children / editor in chief,
William Chester Jordan.
     p. cm.
    Includes bibliographical references (p.109) and index.
    Summary: A guide to the Middle Ages, discussing events, people, and
practices around the world from 500 to 1500.
    ISBN 0-531-11715-4 (lib. bdg.)   0-531-16488-8 (pbk.)
    1. Middle Ages—History Juvenile Literature. [1. Middle Ages, 2. Civi-
lization, Medieval.] I. Jordan, William C., 1948–,
D117.M52 200
956 — dc21   99-30619
                                    CIP

To the Reader

The Middle Ages has generally referred to the history of Europe between the fall of the Roman Empire in A.D. 476 and the Age of Exploration, which led to the discovery of the New World in the late 1400s. In this view of history, the Middle Ages was a "middle" period between ancient and modern times. This is one way of organizing historical periods, but not the only way. For example, the Islamic calendar dates from the hejira, Muhammad's journey from Mecca to Medina. For Europeans, that is the year A.D. 622, but for Muslims, it is the year 1—well into the so-called Middle Ages.

In preparing *The Middle Ages: A Watts Guide for Children,* we have used the term *Middle Ages* in its traditional sense. But because people were living their lives and events were occurring throughout the world during this period, we have tried to highlight some of the political and cultural developments that occurred outside of Europe. The articles refer to three periods within the Middle Ages—early, high, and late. Roughly speaking, the early Middle Ages refers to the years between 476 and 1000; high refers to the years between 1000 and 1350; and late refers to the years between 1350 and 1500.

This volume contains 100 articles carefully chosen to introduce you to the people and events that shaped medieval society. Many of the articles are vividly illustrated with photographs and drawings to attract readers like you. *The Middle Ages* also has some special features you should look for. You may notice words in small capital letters, LIKE THIS. These words are defined in the Glossary at the back of the book.

Most articles end with "See also" references to related articles in the book. Some articles contain sidebars that highlight important events, people, and facts not directly covered in the articles they accompany. If you enjoy this book, and we think you will, turn to the back of the book, where you will find a list of other books on the Middle Ages.

At the very earliest planning stages for *The Middle Ages,* the creators of this book had the good fortune to be able to draw on the services of two young readers. Hannah Meagan Clements and Elliot N. Creager agreed to read several articles and comment on them. Hannah and Elliot also saw some mock-ups of the illustrated pages. They responded enthusiastically. A thousand thanks for their work.

William Chester Jordan
Princeton, New Jersey

Agriculture

Agriculture is the growing of crops and the raising of farm animals. In the Middle Ages, farmers grew crops to feed their families and their animals. They raised animals for food and clothing materials, and some farmers also grew crops to sell or trade.

Farmers grew many different types of crops, including fruits, wheat, and other grains. The choice of crops depended on climate, type of soil, and the usual amount of rainfall in a region. Timing was critical. Farmers divided their fields into sections. Some fields were planted in spring for a fall harvest; others were planted in fall for a spring harvest. Still others were left fallow, or unplanted. By leaving some fields fallow, farmers gave the soil a chance to recover its nutrients and save its moisture.

Farmers used tools and farm animals to help with their work. To prepare the soil for planting, oxen or horses pulled plows across the fields. When the crops, such as wheat, were ready for harvesting, the farmer cut them, usually with a scythe—a large curved blade with a long wooden handle. Then the wheat was threshed—beaten so that the seeds were separated from the stalks or husks.

Animals were used for more than simply to help with farm work. Herders raised cattle, sheep, and goats for the meat and milk they provided and also for their hides and wool, which were used to make clothing. Some farmers also kept horses for transportation.

Methods of farming improved throughout the Middle Ages. New technology enabled farmers to work more efficiently and to produce more crops. But agricultural development also had some setbacks. Changes in climate and weather ruined farmlands. Floods and droughts made farming difficult and caused terrible FAMINES. Wars and invasions also destroyed farmland. (See also *Fairs and Markets; Family and Household.*)

In the late summer, farmers harvested their grain using curved blades called hand sickles. The grain was then gathered into bundles called sheaves and loaded onto a wooden cart for transport.

Alhambra

The Alhambra is a palace located in the city of Granada in southern Spain. The city's Moorish rulers lived in the Alhambra, which was built beginning in the 1200s. The name of the palace comes from the color of its outer walls, which are red. The MOORS called it *qal at al-Hamra,* meaning "the red castle," and the Spanish called it Alhambra. Many people consider it the outstanding example of medieval Islamic architecture.

The Alhambra has three main sections: a living area for the ruler and his family, a palace complex with great meeting halls, and a fortress with tall watchtowers. In addition, many other buildings, gardens, and parks are located around the palace. Because the Moors came from the desert of northwest Africa, they considered water a luxury. The Alhambra's many pools and fountains are among the palace's main features. (See also *Reconquest of Spain.*)

Thomas Aquinas

Thomas Aquinas was a great THEOLOGIAN, or religious scholar. He was born in 1224 to a noble family in Italy. His family wanted him to become a priest, and when he was only five years old, they sent him to live in a monastery. Young Thomas had other ideas: when he was 20, he joined the religious order of Dominicans. Education was important to the Dominicans, and they lived simple lives of study, prayer, and travel for the purpose of spreading Christianity.

Thomas Aquinas went to Germany and France to study theology. He became a teacher at the University of Paris and wrote about the Bible. He also studied the writings of Aristotle, the ancient Greek PHILOSOPHER. Aquinas agreed with Aristotle that knowledge is gained through the senses and understood by the mind. But he also believed that some knowledge is revealed directly by God. Knowledge gained in this way, he felt, must be the absolute truth. Aquinas's blend of Aristotle's teachings and medieval Christian thinking was part of a system of belief and learning that was called Scholasticism. (See also *Dominic; Monks, Friars, and Nuns.*)

Thomas Aquinas, shown in the center, believed that some knowledge was gained through the senses, but that other knowledge was revealed directly by God.

7

Architecture

Architecture is the art of planning and designing buildings. During the Middle Ages, two architectural styles were dominant in Europe—Romanesque and Gothic. Romanesque was the dominant style from about 1000 to 1150.

Romanesque architecture is identified by several special features. The use of vaults—sections of the high, arched ceiling that was made of stone—required the support of sturdy walls and stone pillars. Architects of the time probably were concerned that window openings would weaken the walls, so they included only very small windows and very few of them. That is why the interiors of Romanesque buildings may appear to be dark and gloomy.

Another important characteristic of Romanesque architecture was the breaking up of the interior space into bays—sections bordered by stone columns. The columns divided the interior at evenly spaced intervals. Stone arches on the ceiling connected the columns. Stone or wooden structures called buttresses provided support on the outside.

The church of St. Sernin, shown here, was built in France in the early 1100s. It has the thick walls and heavy curved arches that are characteristic of Romanesque architecture.

Toward the end of the Romanesque period, Gothic architecture developed in northern France and began to spread throughout Europe. Architects who worked in the Gothic style altered some Romanesque elements to create a new look. For example, they used pointed arches instead of rounded ones. Outside, the supporting structures were set away from the walls but connected to them by stone arms. These supports were called flying buttresses. Pointed arches and flying buttresses enabled builders to make walls higher and thinner and to add huge, magnificent stained-glass windows. The windows—many of which were tall and pointed—and the high, pointed vaults created a sense of movement toward heaven. (See also *Art; Cathedrals and Churches.*)

Armor and Weapons

For knights of the Middle Ages, armor and weapons were essential equipment. The knights used weapons to defend themselves and their lands and to attack their enemies. During battle, knights wore armor to protect themselves against injury from their opponents' weapons.

In the early Middle Ages, men fought on foot, using sharp-edged weapons such as swords and daggers. They wore armor made of tiny steel rings linked together. This armor was called chain mail, and it protected the warriors from their enemies' swords. Lightweight and flexible, chain mail was well suited for fighting on foot.

As weapons and methods of fighting changed, chain mail failed to provide enough protection. The knights had begun to use shafted weapons, such as lances and axes, in addition to swords. A lance is a long, thin wooden pole with a sharp steel point at the end. Knights began to fight on horseback and to wear heavier armor. This heavier armor was made of metal plates that were tied together or attached to the knight's jacket. The horses often wore armor too.

To protect themselves from missile weapons, such as arrows and cannons, knights wore helmets and carried large shields. The early helmets fit over a man's head and had a strip of metal in the front to protect his nose. The knight held a shield in his left hand to protect his left side.

Shields became smaller when the full suit of armor was developed. This armor covered the entire body. Helmets covered not only the head and nose but the whole face. The only openings were two small slits for the eyes and holes for breathing. (See also *Castles and Fortifications; Warfare*.)

As weapons of war became more deadly, knights required stronger armor that protected their entire bodies. Only men on horseback wore full armor because it was too heavy for foot soldiers.

Art

Art in the Middle Ages was closely linked to both religion and architecture. Paintings and sculptures were created to decorate churches and other structures built at that time. These works depicted religious leaders and stories from the Bible.

During the medieval period, there were two main styles of European art—Romanesque and Gothic. The Romanesque style was popular from about 1000 to 1150. Romanesque art could be dramatic and full of emotion. Even when the figures were flat and meant to serve as symbols, a sense of movement could be created by sharp lines and angles.

Many Romanesque painters created their works directly on the walls of churches. The large, flat surfaces were well suited for these MURALS. Artists painted in a technique called fresco, in which paint is applied to wet plaster. As the paint dries, it bonds to the plaster, producing bright colors.

Many works of art created during the Middle Ages depicted stories from the Bible. This painting shows Jesus entering Jerusalem.

Romanesque sculpture features an ancient Roman technique called relief. With this method, figures are carved into walls so that they are raised from the surface. Medieval relief sculptures were used to decorate the walls of churches and cathedrals.

As the Romanesque period was ending, around 1150, the Gothic period began. The most important difference between Gothic and Romanesque art is that Gothic art was more naturalistic. Figures looked like real people with natural expressions and poses.

Gothic artists also painted frescoes on the walls of churches. Other popular forms of Gothic art included paintings on wooden panels—a diptych on two panels, a triptych on three—and magnificent works of stained glass. Like Romanesque sculpture, Gothic sculpture was created to adorn the interior and exterior walls of churches and cathedrals. (See also *Icons; Manuscripts and Books.*)

Arthurian Legends

Since the Middle Ages, tales about King Arthur and his Knights of the Round Table have fascinated and entertained people of all ages. People once believed that the Arthurian legends were true. The stories, which began as folktales, may have been based on the lives of real people, but they changed with each retelling, and they are not historically accurate.

According to some legends, Arthur was the son of a king, although he grew up without knowing about his royal blood. One day it was announced that the rightful heir to the throne was the person who could pull a sword, known as Excalibur, out of the stone in which it had been firmly embedded for many years. Many men tried to remove the sword, but they all failed. Finally young Arthur succeeded in pulling the famous sword from the stone, and he was declared king of England. Arthur later married Guinevere, and they lived in a castle called Camelot.

King Arthur was a great ruler and successfully defended Britain against invaders. His court included noble warriors who came to be known as the Knights of the Round Table. Arthur had decided on the round table to show that no one knight was more valued than another—they were all equal. According to some tales, King Arthur and the Knights of the Round Table had many adventures. One such adventure was the quest for the Holy Grail, the cup that Jesus Christ used at the Last Supper.

After Arthur and his knights returned from their quest, Sir Lancelot fell in love with Queen Guinevere. Angry and disappointed by his friend's betrayal, Arthur sought revenge against Lancelot. While Arthur pursued Lancelot, his son Mordred seized the kingdom. Arthur returned home and fought a battle with his son, in which both men died.

The first literary works about King Arthur came from France in the 1100s. By 1225 there were Norse versions of King Arthur's story as well as versions written in Latin, Italian, Hebrew, and Spanish. The themes that run through all of them are CHIVALRY, courtly love, and the quest for the Holy Grail. (See also *Courtly Love; Literature.*)

King Arthur is shown here introducing Sir Galahad to the other knights.

Aztec Empire

The Aztec Empire was one of the largest civilizations to exist in the Americas in the Middle Ages. The Aztecs settled along the lake shores of central Mexico in the 1200s. At first they were ruled by neighboring tribes, but their advanced farming methods enabled them to become stronger than their neighbors. They built artificial islands, called *chinampas,* in the lake to use for farming. Eventually the people grew numerous and rich enough to found their own CITY-STATE in 1325. It was called Tenochtitlán.

When Tenochtitlán joined with two other cities, the Aztec empire was established. Fierce Aztec warriors conquered territory that eventually stretched as far south as present-day Guatemala. The Aztecs went to war to expand their empire and to capture prisoners to sacrifice to the gods they worshiped.

Religion was a major part of the Aztecs' lives, and human sacrifice was an important part of their religion. Aztec priests would offer a victim's heart to the sun god. These bloody rituals took place in temples on top of huge stone pyramids. From these pyramids, the priests, who were also skilled ASTRONOMERS, studied the stars and the planets. They told the people when to sow crops, when to go to war, and when to offer sacrifices.

Aztec society was divided into several classes. Emperors, government officials, priests, and traders had the most power and privileges. Farmers, serfs, and slaves had the least power. The crowded Aztec cities had not only pyramids and temples for worship but also zoos and parks for leisure and streets and canals for transportation. Each day, thousands of people came to the cities to trade their goods, which included CACAO beans, cotton, jaguar pelts, and rubber.

In 1519 the Spanish CONQUISTADOR Hernán Cortés landed in Mexico and began to march toward the Aztec capital. His troops were supported by native people who had been conquered by the Aztecs and were angry at having to pay taxes to the empire. According to legend, the Aztec emperor believed that Cortés was the god Quetzalcoatl. After two years of warfare and outbreaks of smallpox and other European diseases, the Aztec Empire was destroyed. The Spaniards then built Mexico City on the ruins of Tenochtitlán.

Although the empire was destroyed, Aztec culture is still very strong in Mexico. The word *Mexico* comes from *Mexica,* another word for Aztec. Aztec foods—such as tortillas, tacos, and chocolate—are still served today, and the words *avocado, tomato,* and *coyote* come from Nahuatl, the Aztec language.

Thomas Becket

Thomas Becket, born in London in 1118, became the chancellor of England and later the archbishop of Canterbury. As chancellor, Becket supervised the chancery, the department of government that wrote important documents and letters for the king. As the archbishop of Canterbury, Becket was the highest church official in England.

After his appointment as chancellor, Becket became the close friend and adviser of King Henry II. Henry made Becket archbishop and expected him to continue supporting royal policies. But Becket began to disagree with the king.

Becket is shown here being attacked by the king's men as he prayed in Canterbury Cathedral.

Henry wanted more control over the church; Becket thought that this was a bad idea. The king became angry, and Becket left the country for several years. In his absence, Henry asked the archbishop of York to crown the prince as heir to the throne. The right to perform that ceremony belonged to the archbishop of Canterbury. Soon afterward, Becket returned to England and EXCOMMUNICATED the men who had helped crown the prince. This made King Henry so angry that he hinted that he wished to have Becket killed. Four of the king's knights killed Thomas Becket in Canterbury Cathedral. Becket's murder caused an uproar in Europe, and three years after his death, he was declared a saint. (See also *Chaucer*.)

Bernard of Clairvaux

Bernard was born in 1090 near Dijon, France. In his early 20s, he joined a small Cistercian monastery. The Cistercians were trying to bring back some of the Church practices that had disappeared, such as living a simple life of poverty and prayer.

After three years Bernard was asked to be the leader of a new monastery at Clairvaux. He served there for the next 38 years. During that time, he wrote many letters, SERMONS, and HYMNS, and the monastery became the most important one in the Cistercian order.

Bernard attracted many new followers. He was a persuasive speaker and encouraged many people to join the Second Crusade, one of a series of holy wars against the enemies of the Christian Church. He founded almost 70 new monasteries and became the adviser to the pope. In 1174, Bernard was declared a saint.

Black Death

The Black Death, also known as the plague, was a disease that killed millions of people during the Middle Ages. Between 1347 and 1351, the disease spread throughout Europe, killing between 25 and 45 percent of the population. The Black Death was the greatest natural disaster in European history.

Plague is a deadly and highly contagious disease. It is caused by BACTERIA usually found in fleas and the small animals, especially rats, on which they feed. But sometimes fleas infect humans with the bacteria, and when that happens, the disease can spread quickly.

There are two main types of plague: bubonic plague and pneumonic plague. Both types occurred during the Black Death. Bubonic plague is spread when the bacteria infect the blood, causing swellings and purplish blotches from broken blood vessels. If the bacteria attack the lungs, pneumonic plague develops. This type of plague spreads as easily as the common cold. No cure existed for either type of plague. About 50 percent of the people with bubonic plague died; the pneumonic plague killed nearly all of its victims within a few days.

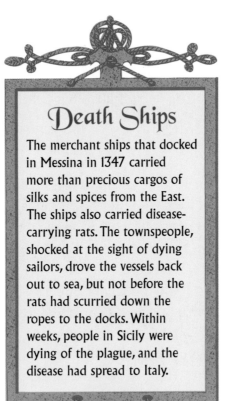

Death Ships

The merchant ships that docked in Messina in 1347 carried more than precious cargos of silks and spices from the East. The ships also carried disease-carrying rats. The townspeople, shocked at the sight of dying sailors, drove the vessels back out to sea, but not before the rats had scurried down the ropes to the docks. Within weeks, people in Sicily were dying of the plague, and the disease had spread to Italy.

The Black Death reached Europe aboard merchant ships that unknowingly carried infected rats. In Western Europe, the disease first appeared in Messina, a seaport on the island of Sicily. It quickly spread throughout Italy and then northward to France. In Paris there were reports of 800 people dying each day.

In just a few years the Black Death had spread to Spain, Germany, England, Scandinavia, Russia, and even as far away as Greenland. It also caused millions of deaths among the Muslim populations of North Africa and the Near East.

In addition to its enormous death toll, the plague had other important effects on medieval society. Many people thought that the Black Death was a punishment from God and became more religious than before. The plague also seriously affected the economy of medieval Europe. The loss of so many people left too few workers. Farms were abandoned, creating serious food shortages, and fewer craftsworkers in the cities meant that fewer products were available to buy. Although these shortages caused prices to rise, the high demand for workers led to higher wages, which in turn raised the standard of living for many who had survived. In the end, the Black Death played a major role in Europe's move from a medieval society to a modern one. (See also *Medicine*.)

The Black Death first reached Western Europe when a ship carrying infected rats docked in the port of Messina on the Mediterranean island of Sicily in 1347. Within five years, the Black Death had spread across all of Europe, killing millions.

Byzantine Empire

The Byzantine Empire is the name given to the Roman Empire's eastern territories after the western territories had been conquered. In the year 330, Emperor Constantine I made the city of Byzantium a new capital of the Roman Empire and renamed it Constantinople after himself. Constantinople became a rich port city, where silks and spices from Asia were traded for furs and slaves from Europe. After Constantine's death in 337, the Roman Empire was divided into two parts—the Eastern (Byzantine) Empire and the Western Empire. Although the Western Empire collapsed during the 400s, the Byzantine Empire survived for another 1,000 years.

The Byzantine Empire reached its greatest size when the emperor Justinian recaptured much of the former Western Roman Empire, including parts of southern and eastern Europe, northern Africa, and the Middle East. During his rule Justinian collected and organized Roman laws for use in his empire. These laws, known as the Justinian Code, became the basis of many modern European legal systems. Although Justinian expanded and fortified the empire, his improvements were expensive.

After Justinian's death in 565, the empire was unable to hold on to many of its recaptured territories. Lombards from Germany captured parts of Italy. Slavs from Eastern Europe seized the Balkan Peninsula. A long war with Persia continued to weaken the Byzantine Empire. The Persians even laid SIEGE to Constantinople. The emperor Heraclius defeated them in 628, but the empire then lost Syria, Palestine, and Egypt to Arab Muslims.

Religion was very important in the Byzantine Empire. The empire's founder, Constantine I, was the first Roman emperor who was a Christian. By the time of Heraclius, some people believed that the empire was suffering defeats because God was displeased with religious images, called icons, that Eastern Christians displayed and revered. A dispute arose between those who wanted the icons destroyed (iconoclasts) and those who wanted to keep them. Eventually the iconoclasts lost, and icons became an important and lasting part of the Eastern Orthodox Church.

From the 800s to the 1000s, the empire once again expanded as Byzantine armies reconquered territory that had been lost to the Arabs. During this time, Constantinople became a center of science and the arts. MISSIONARIES helped to reduce the threat of invasion by Slavs and other Eastern European peoples by converting them to Christianity.

However, frequent rebellions and wars caused the empire to decline in influence during the 1000s. After the Muslim Turks attacked

Empress Theodora (center) was the wife of Byzantine emperor Justinian I. When a revolt in Constantinople threatened her husband's control of the empire, Theodora persuaded Justinian to remain in the city and crush the rebellion.

Constantinople, Emperor Alexius I Comnenus asked the Christians in Western Europe to help him defend his empire. The wars that Western Christians undertook became known as the Crusades.

In the long run, the Crusades did more to harm the Byzantine Empire than to help it, for the Crusaders PILLAGED both Muslim and Christian cities. In 1204, during the Fourth Crusade, Crusaders supported merchants from the Italian city of Venice and helped conquer Constantinople. The Byzantines recaptured Constantinople from the Western Christians, but war had left the empire weaker than ever.

In the 1300s, Muslim Turks known as Ottomans were threatening Constantinople. Byzantine emperors again pleaded for the protection of the West, but they failed to receive the help they sought. In 1453 the Ottoman leader Mehmed II conquered Constantinople. The last Byzantine emperor died defending Constantinople. Mehmed made the city—now known as Istanbul—the capital of the Ottoman Empire.

The 1,000-year rule of the Byzantine Empire served as a link between the ancient and modern worlds. The empire helped preserve the culture and ideas of ancient Greece and Rome, much of which otherwise might have been lost. (See also *Crusades; Eastern Europe*.)

Castles and Fortifications

Fighting was a part of everyday life during the Middle Ages as battles were waged over power, land, and religion. Castles and other fortifications were very important during these battles for the protection they provided. Behind castle walls, knights and soldiers defended themselves, their families, and their possessions. Many towns were also surrounded by strong walls to prevent attacks by raiders.

Many factors were considered in the planning of fortifications—the nature of the site, the types of attacks that were most likely to occur, and the building materials that were available. Labor and other resources also had to be considered. The designs and techniques used to build castles and fortifications changed over time.

During the early Middle Ages, height was an important factor. Steep hills or cliffsides were well suited for castles. One reason was that they were difficult for enemies to climb. In addition, those who defended a castle on high ground had the advantage of gravity. Because of gravity, the defenders' arrows, stones, and other objects traveled farther, gathered more speed, and had greater impact when they hit a target. Gravity also worked against enemies by making it more difficult for them to hurl rocks or shoot arrows up into the castle.

Many of the earliest castles were made of wood because people could build and rebuild them quickly and easily. But during the 1100s, more powerful weapons were introduced that could severely damage wooden castles. In addition, wood became scarce in Europe as the population grew and people used it to build more ships and houses. In place of wood, castle builders began to use stone, which was not only stronger than wood but fireproof as well.

During the late Middle Ages, new weapons were developed that could hurl stones weighing hundreds of pounds. If a wall—even a stone wall—was hit repeatedly with such stones, it would eventually crumble. Castle builders responded by making the walls thicker. They also began to use a circular design for the towers because rounded towers were better able to withstand repeated blows.

With the invention of the cannon, however, these improvements became less effective. By the late 1300s, cannonballs could cause serious damage, even to the strongest castle walls. Even castles built on high hills were at risk because cannonballs could travel great distances. While castle walls and other fortifications were becoming stronger, advancements in weaponry made them less and less secure. (See also *Architecture; Warfare.*)

Some castles (such as this one) were surrounded by deep, water-filled ditches called moats. A drawbridge was lowered to allow visitors to enter the castle. Medieval castles were protected from enemy attack by high, thick walls. Battlements—short walls with indentations—enabled guards to keep watch and to shoot arrows at approaching enemies.

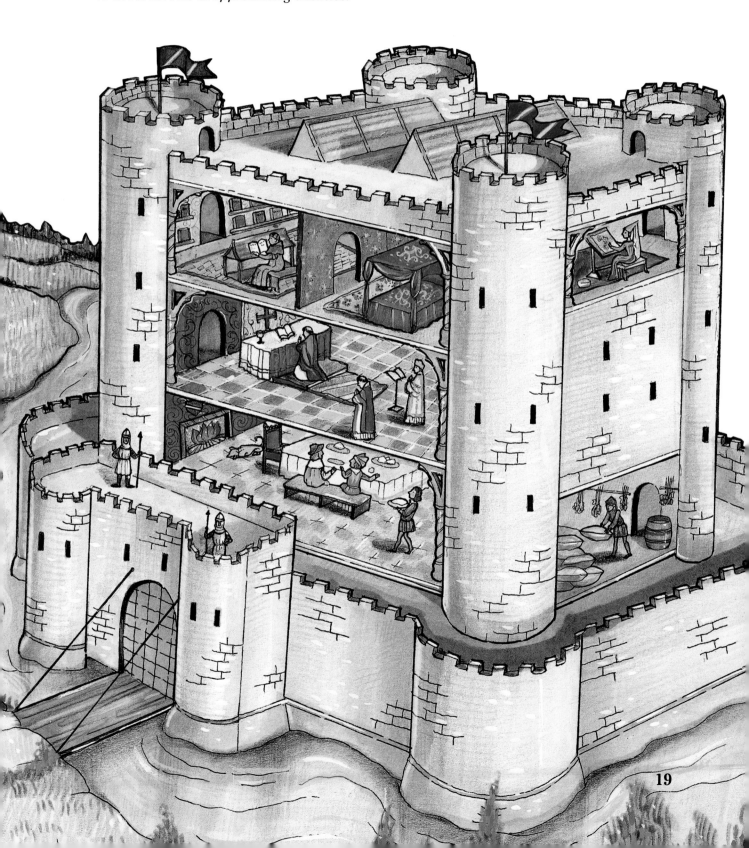

Cathedrals and Churches

Many churches and cathedrals were built during the Middle Ages. Cathedrals are usually much larger than ordinary churches, and they contain the bishop's throne. A cathedral usually is the largest church in the diocese, or district under the supervision of a bishop. The construction of a cathedral took many years—sometimes centuries—to complete and required donations from almost everyone in the community.

The designs of early Christian churches were based on the ancient Roman basilica, or public hall. These large, rectangular buildings were constructed according to a simple plan. At one end of the building was the apse—a semicircular area with a high, vaulted ceiling. Throughout the Middle Ages, however, architects changed and improved their designs. Many cathedrals and churches became impressive buildings that today are also considered great works of art.

The early Byzantine churches were square, featuring a floor plan that resembled the Greek cross—a symbol whose upright beam was the same length as the cross beam. Byzantine architects later developed a unique style by adding domed roofs and mosaic wall decorations. Mosaics are pictures made from tiny pieces of glass or stone that are set in mortar, a cementlike material. After the year 800, the most common church design featured a small dome in the center and other domes at the corners.

The most spectacular Byzantine church is Hagia Sophia in Constantinople. Built in less than six years in the mid-500s, it has a huge central dome. The interior is decorated with many colorful mosaics, which were added later. The dome and the light shining through it create a sense of vast openness.

In the 1000s and early 1100s, European churches were built in the Romanesque style. This type of architecture, which was also based on ancient Roman designs, had rounded arches and thick, massive walls. Instead of wooden roofs, which could easily catch fire and burn, builders used heavy stone vaults—sections of ceiling arches. The vaults were supported by sturdy columns that divided the interior space into sections called bays.

Between 1150 and 1300, many Gothic churches and cathedrals were built in Western Europe. Buildings in this architectural style had pointed arches, and they were taller and had thinner walls than those in the Romanesque style. On the outside of Gothic cathedrals, stone structures called flying buttresses were used to support the high interior walls. The Gothic style also included large stained-glass windows. People still worship in many of the churches and cathedrals that were built during the Middle Ages. The beauty of these buildings attracts thousands of visitors as well. (See also *Architecture; Byzantine Empire; Christianity.*)

France's Chartres Cathedral, shown here, has more than 180 stained-glass windows. The multicolored glass in these windows filters the light coming in, giving it a jewel-like quality.

Charlemagne

Charlemagne, born around 742, was one of the greatest military leaders of the Middle Ages. During his reign, he expanded the Frankish kingdom and became the first medieval emperor in Western Europe. He also helped to revive the political and cultural life of his kingdom.

Charlemagne was the grandson of Charles Martel and the son of Pepin III the Short. Charles Martel united the Frankish lands. Pepin succeeded him, became king of the Franks, and founded the royal family known as the Carolingians. After Pepin's death, Charlemagne and his brother Carloman shared the rule. When Carloman died three years later, Charlemagne became sole ruler of the kingdom. During his reign, he conquered much of Europe. In Rome, on Christmas Day in 800, Pope Leo III placed a crown on Charlemagne's head and declared him emperor. Although his conquests gave him great power, Charlemagne allowed his conquered subjects to keep their own laws and traditions. But if they were PAGANS, he made them become Christians.

According to Frankish custom, Charlemagne's three sons were to share the rule when he died. But only one of those sons, Louis I the Pious, was alive when Charlemagne died in 814, and he became emperor. (See also *Holy Roman Empire; Papacy.*)

Chaucer

Geoffrey Chaucer, born around 1340, was the greatest English writer of the Middle Ages. His most famous work is *Canterbury Tales.* Through his writing, Chaucer helped increase the acceptance of English as a literary language. His wit, wisdom, and deep understanding of human nature gained him a reputation as one of the best-loved writers of all time.

He was the son of a wealthy London wine merchant and was working for one of England's royal families by the age of 17. He had many other jobs as well, including one as a clerk for the wool trade and similar work for several royal estates. Even with these jobs, however, Chaucer found time to write many important works, including *Troilus and Criseyde,* a tragic love story.

Chaucer wrote *Canterbury Tales* during the last years of his life. This collection of stories involves a pilgrimage to the SHRINE of Saint Thomas Becket at Canterbury Cathedral. The pilgrims in the story—a knight, a parson, a merchant, a widow, a plowman, and others—come from all walks of life and represent the whole range of medieval society. (See also *Literature.*)

China

In the years before the Middle Ages, China was a divided country. Then, in 581, the Sui DYNASTY was established. Although it lasted only until 618, the Sui dynasty unified China.

The T'ang dynasty followed the Sui and remained in power from 618 to 906. During this time, China enjoyed great prosperity and cultural growth. Ch'ang-an, the T'ang capital, was the world's largest city and attracted many important people from throughout Asia and the Mediterranean region. Some of China's best-known poets wrote during the T'ang dynasty. Gunpowder—which was used for fireworks—was invented during the T'ang dynasty.

The T'ang dynasty ended after two rebellions weakened the empire, and a brief period known as the Five Dynasties followed from 907 to 960. During the struggle that accompanied the Five Dynasties, ten independent states were established. The Five Dynasties period ended when the Song dynasty reunified China. During the Song period, which lasted from 960 to 1279, literature, PHILOSOPHY, and the arts flourished. The Chinese developed MOVABLE TYPE around 1050—about 400 years before it was used in Europe—and more and more people learned to read and write.

In the 1200s, Mongol warriors invaded China. First led by Genghis Khan and later by his grandson Kublai Khan, the Mongols eventually conquered the entire region.

In the mid-1300s, the Mongols were driven out of China and the Ming dynasty was established. With this new dynasty, which ruled from 1268 to 1644, came a revival of Chinese influence in Asia. (See also *Mongol Empire.*)

During the rule of the T'ang dynasty, China enjoyed a long period of peace and prosperity. The emperor is shown here on his throne.

The Great Wall of China

The protective wall that runs along China's northern and northwestern borders was begun around 221 B.C. It is made of earth and stone. Builders constructed watchtowers two bowshots apart, enabling archers to defend the entire wall. During the Ming dynasty in the late Middle Ages, the wall was repaired and lengthened. When the work was finished, the Great Wall extended for about 1,500 miles through forests, over mountains, and along riverbanks.

Christianity

Christianity, the faith based on the life and teachings of Jesus Christ, became the dominant religion of Europe during the Middle Ages. It is one of the world's major religions today. Like Jews and Muslims, Christians believe in one God, and that he created the universe. Christians also believe that God exists in three forms: the Father, the Son (Jesus Christ), and the Holy Spirit.

During his lifetime, Jesus preached in Jerusalem, where he attracted a large following. Roman officials, fearing Jesus' growing influence, charged him with treason and CRUCIFIED him. For almost 300 years, Christians were persecuted by the Roman emperors. Then, in 312, before the Middle Ages began, the Roman emperor Constantine I permitted Christians to worship freely. By the end of the 300s, Christianity was the official religion of the Roman Empire.

In 395, the Roman Empire was divided into two parts—Western and Eastern. Leadership of the Christian Church was also divided. Rome became the center of the Western or Latin Christian Church and was headed by the bishop of Rome, later known as the pope. Constantinople became the center of the Eastern or Greek Christian Church. The highest official of the Eastern Church was the patriarch, or bishop, of Constantinople.

In the early Middle Ages, after the fall of the Western Roman Empire, the pope was the most powerful person in Europe. He had authority over both religious and many political matters. In the late 700s the pope strengthened the Church's ties with the Franks, a powerful Germanic people in the region of present-day France and Germany. During the reign of the Frankish ruler Charlemagne, these ties became even stronger. Charlemagne's goal was to unite the Frankish empire in Christianity, and in 800, Pope Leo III crowned Charlemagne "Emperor of the Romans."

In the 1000s and 1100s, popes and emperors quarreled bitterly about their powers, especially when they disagreed about the appointment of bishops. This long struggle, known as the Investiture Controversy, led to the strengthening of papal authority and a weakening of the authority of other rulers.

The power of the papacy remained strong for the next 200 years. But in the early 1300s, problems arose once again when European rulers tried to control the pope's political power. In 1309, a French pope ruled the Church from Avignon, France. The papacy returned to Rome in 1377, but the following year, two rival popes were elected—one in Rome and one in Avignon. This division, which lasted for 40 years,

This painting shows Pope Leo III crowning Charlemagne "Emperor of the Romans." During his long reign, Charlemagne promoted Christianity throughout the Frankish empire.

was known as the Great Schism and resulted in a loss of power for the papacy.

While the Western Christian Church in Rome was becoming more powerful, the Eastern Christian Church was weakening. The Byzantine Empire itself was increasingly under attack by Muslims. Russian churches, loyal to the Eastern Christian patriarch, remained independent. By the end of the Middle Ages, the center of the Russian church had moved north to Moscow. When Constantinople finally fell to the Ottoman Turks in 1453, Russian Christians named Moscow the "third Rome"—after the great Christian centers in ancient Rome and Constantinople. (See also *Crusades; Holy Roman Empire.*)

Cities and Towns

The growth of medieval cities and towns was influenced by the history, geography, and economy of each region. Some medieval cities developed where ancient Greek and Roman cities had once existed. New buildings were sometimes constructed on the foundations of old buildings that had been destroyed by wars.

Towns sprang up at or near rivers and at major crossroads. Some developed around important existing buildings, such as a church, a monastery, or a castle. Others—such as the great Islamic centers of Baghdad and Cairo—were carefully planned.

Whether planned or unplanned, medieval cities and towns had important buildings at their centers. In European cities, these buildings were cathedrals or town halls. In Islamic cities, the central buildings included the MOSQUE and the marketplace. Most medieval towns developed neighborhoods, often based on religious or ethnic background. Streets were usually narrow and suitable only for pedestrians and riders. Carts and other wheeled traffic used the fewer wide roads that existed.

A major feature of most medieval towns was the protective walls that surrounded them. These defensive walls were constructed to help shield the town from invaders and thieves. Early protective walls were made of wood. Stone walls later replaced the wooden ones. Sections of these stone walls still exist in many places. (See also *Fairs and Markets; Trade.*)

Medieval cities were built around important buildings. They were centers of trade, and many were surrounded by protective walls.

Clare of Assisi

Clare of Assisi, born around 1193, organized a religious community for women. The group came to be known as the Order of Saint Clare. They were also called the Poor Clares because, like the Franciscan friars, they took a vow of poverty. This vow meant that they refused to earn money or to own property. Clare felt that poverty freed people to focus all of their attention on God.

Clare became a nun against the wishes of her wealthy parents. With the help of Francis of Assisi, the founder of the Franciscan order, Clare established the Poor Clares at the church of San Damiano in 1212. She became abbess (leader) of the order. Clare wanted her nuns to travel through the countryside spreading Christianity, but the Church would not allow them to live outside a convent.

Just two years after Clare's death, the Church officially declared her a saint. By 1400, her order had grown to about 15,000 members in 400 convents. (See also *Monks, Friars, and Nuns.*)

Constantinople

In ancient times, Constantinople was called Byzantium and was an important trading center. Then, in the early 300s, the Roman emperor Constantine renamed it Constantinople and made it the capital of the Byzantine Empire—the "New Rome" of the East.

Located on the waterway that connects the Black Sea to the Mediterranean and Aegean seas, Constantinople was a natural harbor on the major trade routes of the East. Because the city was surrounded by water on three sides and a huge fortification on the fourth, it was well protected against attack. By the early 500s, it was already the largest city in the Mediterranean, with a population of about 500,000. Constantinople served as the religious center of the Eastern Orthodox Church and a cultural bridge between the ancient and modern worlds.

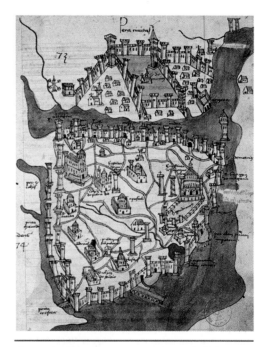

Constantinople was surrounded by water on three sides, as shown by this map drawn in 1420.

Constantinople usually fought off attempted invasions, but in 1453 the city fell to the Ottoman Turks. Now known as Istanbul, it is still an important city. (See also *Byzantine Empire.*)

Costume and Clothing

Clothing in the Middle Ages varied greatly from region to region and even from community to community. The variations sprang from differences in climate, religion, social status, occupation, culture, and the availability of fabrics. One element that was common to almost all medieval cultures was a head covering. Head coverings included veils, turbans, hats, and hoods. For many years, clothing styles were based on custom and tradition. They changed, however, as trade expanded and people were exposed to new and different styles.

In the Byzantine Empire, clothing reflected the styles of ancient Rome. Both men and women wore tunics, which were knee length for soldiers and workingmen and floor length for women and officials. The Byzantines obtained fine materials, such as silk, from Asia, so the clothing of the Byzantine upper classes was often made of silky fabrics. Some garments were accented with elaborate embroidery or gemstones.

Islamic clothing was influenced by pre-Islamic Arabia, Greece, Rome, and central Asia. In Islamic culture, clothing was meant only to hide the body. Muslims wore simple clothing—a tunic worn over a shirt, with an overgarment for colder weather. As people became wealthier, however, their clothing became fancier.

In Western Europe, clothing had great social significance. In the early Middle Ages, Europeans wore simple garments but added their own finery, such as jewelry and fur. As trade expanded and merchants brought fine fabrics back to Europe from the East, wealthy people used these fine fabrics for their clothes. Even poor people and peasants made holiday costumes of the finest materials they could afford. (See also *Armor and Weapons*.)

During the Middle Ages, clothing indicated the social status of the wearer. This illustration shows a nobleman and his wife standing before a bishop and a young monk.

Courtly Love

Courtly love describes the rules of behavior in medieval Europe between a man and a woman who were in love. The man, who was usually a knight, expressed his undying devotion to the woman he desired. He offered to be her servant and to prove his dedication by performing brave deeds for her.

The woman was usually of noble birth, sometimes belonging to a higher social class than the knight. She might also be married to someone other than the knight. During the Middle Ages, noble marriages were often arranged for business reasons rather than because the two people loved each other. Courtly love, then, was the only romantic love for many of the noble class.

The ideals of courtly love were described in the lyrics of the troubadours—poet-singers of southern France beginning in the 1000s. They traveled throughout Western Europe, entertaining the nobility with their songs. Courtly love became a major theme in European art and literature.

Courtly love was a favorite subject of many medieval authors, including Dante, who is shown here with his beloved Beatrice.

Many medieval authors, including Chaucer and Dante, wrote about courtly love. Some of the traditions of courtly love, such as love at first sight and forbidden love, have survived and can be found in the music and literature of today. (See also *Nobles and Knights*.)

Crusades

The Crusades were a succession of wars undertaken by Christians to recapture the Holy Land in Palestine from Muslims. During the eight major Crusades, Christians from Western Europe fought Muslims for control of the land that was sacred to three of the world's great religions—Christianity, Islam, and Judaism.

During the 600s, Muslims captured Palestine from the Eastern Christians in the Byzantine Empire. Until the 1000s, the new Muslim rulers allowed Christians to visit the Holy Land. Then the Muslim Turks blocked the usual pilgrimage routes and attacked the Byzantine Empire. Emperor Alexius I Comnenus asked the leader of the Roman Catholic Church, Pope Urban II, to raise an army to help defend the Byzantine Empire. Urban agreed because he wanted to regain control of the Holy Land and unite the divided powers of Western Europe under his leadership.

The pope called for Europeans to organize an army to defend the Byzantine Empire and to liberate Jerusalem from the Muslims. He promised God's forgiveness of past sins to all who joined the army. Believing that it was God's will to defeat the Muslims, thousands of people hurried to join. The word *crusade* comes from the Latin word for "cross," and the Crusaders wore crosses on their clothes.

The Crusade took several years to organize. Meanwhile, some people rushed ahead. A preacher called Peter the Hermit led a peasant army to the Holy Land. Many in this group had neither food nor adequate weapons and were killed or enslaved by the Muslims.

The first official Crusade was fought by well-trained knights from France and Normandy. They united with Byzantine forces and won many battles against the Muslims. By 1099 they had captured Jerusalem, their main goal, and established four Crusader states. The Knights Templars and other orders were established to help protect the Holy Land.

The Crusaders were unable to hold on to the reconquered land permanently. The Second Crusade started in 1147, after Muslims attacked Crusader states under Christian control. Armies from Western Europe were defeated by the Muslims, and many of the Crusaders were killed or sold into slavery.

The Third Crusade was called around 1187 to protect the crusader states from further defeat. Saladin, a powerful VIZIER, had united the Muslim people in the Holy Land, led them to victory over the Christian armies, and captured Jerusalem. Only a few cities remained under Christian control. The Third Crusade failed to retake Jerusalem, but King Richard the Lionhearted of England negotiated an agreement to allow pilgrims to visit the city.

Many people were killed during the Crusades, and those who were captured in battle were often enslaved.

The Fourth Crusade was called in 1198 to recapture Jerusalem, but the Crusaders became involved in other battles that distracted them from their holy mission. They agreed to help the Greek prince Alexius claim the throne of the Byzantine Empire in exchange for his help in reconquering the Holy Land. Once in power, Alexius was unable to keep his promise, so the Crusaders plundered his capital city of Constantinople.

Around 1228, Holy Roman Emperor Frederick II successfully regained Jerusalem for a period of ten years. What is especially noteworthy is that Frederick accomplished this by DIPLOMACY rather than by battle. Several other major Crusades to the East occurred in the later 1200s. Some were very large, but the results were mixed. The last Crusader outpost fell to the Muslims in 1291.

The Crusades failed to accomplish their two main goals—regaining permanent control of the Holy Land and protecting the Byzantine Empire. The Crusaders actually weakened the Byzantine Empire and eased the way for the Ottoman Turks, who conquered it in 1453. On the other hand, the Crusaders accomplished something they had never anticipated. As a result of the Crusades, the trade of goods and ideas between Western Europe and the Middle East increased dramatically, greatly influencing the history of both regions. (See also *Papacy; Warfare.*)

Dante

Dante Alighieri is considered one of the greatest writers of the Middle Ages. Born in 1265 in Florence, Italy, Dante had lost both parents by the time he was a teenager. As was the custom of the time, Dante's family chose his future wife, whom he married when he was 20. Although married to Gemma Donati, Dante wrote beautiful poems about another woman, Beatrice Portinari, whom he passionately loved.

In Dante's time Florence was divided between two political groups, which were called the Whites and the Blacks (from the shirts/uniforms they wore). While Dante was away on a mission for the Whites, the Blacks took over Florence. They warned Dante that if he tried to return to the city, he would be killed. So Dante was forced to stay away from his beloved Florence for the rest of his life.

During this period of EXILE, Dante wrote the *Divine Comedy*. In this epic poem, he tells of an imaginary journey through Hell, Purgatory, and Heaven. Christians believe that when people die, their souls go to one of these places. Dante included his political beliefs in the poem. He placed his enemies in Hell and his friends in Heaven. Dante's *Divine Comedy* became one of the most celebrated works of world literature.

The poet Dante Alighieri is shown here holding a copy of his epic poem the Divine Comedy.

Dominic

Dominic was born in 1170 in Castile, a region of northern Spain. He studied THEOLOGY and PHILOSOPHY, and in 1206, he went to southern France on a mission to preach against HERESY. Ten years later, the pope granted approval for Dominic to establish the Order of Friars Preachers, or Dominicans.

Those who joined took a vow of poverty. They could not earn money or own property. Dominic believed that education was the key to preventing the spread of heresy, and he sent new members of the order to study theology in universities. Some members of the order became the most influential teachers of the Middle Ages.

Realizing the importance of religious women in the Church, Dominic founded many convents for nuns. He died in Italy in 1221 and was declared a saint 13 years later.

Dracula

Dracula, whose real name was Vlad III Dracul, was a freedom fighter and ruthless leader in the late Middle Ages. His father was Vlad II Dracul. (*Dracul* means "devil"; *Dracula* means "little devil.") Dracula's father was the prince of Walachia, a region in Eastern Europe. After Vlad II was overthrown by Hungarian forces in 1447, young Dracula announced that he was the new prince. But Dracula's reign lasted only a few months. Pro-Hungarian forces soon drove him out of Walachia and kept him out for eight years.

When Dracula returned, he joined the Hungarians and began the reign of terror for which he is remembered. He burned villages and killed thousands of his enemies by impaling them—lifting them onto long, sharp stakes that pierced their bodies. This cruel method of execution earned him the name of Vlad Tepes, or Vlad the Impaler. Dracula was killed in battle in 1476. His reputation for cruelty outlived him, and in 1897 he became the model for the vampire Count Dracula in Bram Stoker's famous novel. (See also *Eastern Europe*.)

Vlad Tepes's infamous cruelty may have inspired Bram Stoker to write a novel about a vampire named Count Dracula.

Eleanor of Aquitaine

Eleanor of Aquitaine was one of the most famous women of the Middle Ages. Born in France around 1122, she inherited great landholdings from her father when she was about 15. That same year, she married Louis, the 16-year-old son of the king of France. When his father died a year later, he became King Louis VII, and Eleanor became queen.

In 1147, Eleanor went with her husband on the Second Crusade to the Holy Land. Problems developed in the marriage, however, and it was ANNULLED. Eleanor then married Henry Plantagenet. When he became King Henry II of England in 1154, Eleanor once again became a queen.

Eleanor and Henry had eight children, and she worked hard to make her family powerful. When Henry II died in 1189, their son Richard I the Lionhearted became king. Richard spent several years fighting in the Third Crusade, and during that time, Eleanor helped govern the kingdom. When Richard died in 1199, Eleanor helped her youngest son, John, succeed his brother to the throne. In addition, two of Eleanor's daughters became queens.

Eastern Europe

Eastern Europe refers to the medieval lands bordered by Germany (to the west), the Byzantine Empire (to the south), and Asia (to the east). Eastern Europe was distinguished from Western Europe by its large Slavic population and by its later conversion to Christianity.

Slavs made up the largest population in Eastern Europe during the Middle Ages. They lived near the Black Sea until the mid-500s. Then tribes known as Turkic Avars conquered the lands around the Black Sea, forcing the Slavs to move elsewhere. These migrating Slavic tribes brought their culture and traditions to Eastern Europe.

The Slavic language spread into many parts of Eastern Europe. As Slavic tribes separated and settled in different communities, their language gradually changed from a single language to the dozen or so different Slavic-based languages that are spoken today. The first written Slavic language was created using Greek-like letters. It is still used in many modern Eastern European countries, including Russia, Ukraine, Belarus, and Bulgaria.

This first Slavic alphabet was created to help Slavs convert to the Christianity practiced in the Byzantine Empire. Two monks—Cyril and Methodios, brothers who were later declared saints—created the alphabet in the 800s. They used it to translate Christian writings into the Slavic language.

Many of the peoples of Eastern Europe were converted to Christianity through the influence of these two monks and the leadership of several generations of Christian kings. By the 1000s, all Slavic lands had been converted and brought into the group of Christian nations known as Christendom.

Although there are many similarities among the peoples of Eastern Europe, some important differences exist. Most people in Hungary trace their origins back to a NOMADIC people known as Magyars, who were not Slavs. Romanians claim descent from ancient Roman immigrants. In addition, certain Eastern European nations—such as Bohemia, Slovakia, Hungary, and Poland—adopted the Roman form of Christianity. People in these nations use the Latin alphabet instead of the Cyrillic alphabet (named for the monk Cyril) used by the Slavs who converted to Eastern Christianity.

Unity Breaks Down

In the late 800s, Slavic tribes united to form the Great Moravian Empire under Prince Svatopluk. The empire controlled a large part of central Europe. Soon afterward, however, the empire was conquered by the Magyars (ancestors of the Hungarians).

More than 1,000 years later, Slavs once again united to form the nations of Poland, Czechoslovakia, and Yugoslavia. But unity broke down in the 1990s, causing civil wars in parts of the region.

Fairs and Markets

Medieval fairs were events to which merchants sometimes came from great distances to trade their goods. Fairs were temporary, lasting from one day to several weeks, and occurred at specific times of the year. Markets were similar to fairs, but they were local, often weekly, events intended for the buying and selling of goods among ordinary townspeople. Both fairs and markets helped the economy during the Middle Ages.

In the early Middle Ages, trade was usually carried out over short distances because travel was difficult and dangerous. Over time, as travel became easier and safer, fairs became more frequent. The goods traded at early European fairs consisted mostly of agricultural products—grain, hides, wool, and animals. At later fairs, manufactured and imported goods were also traded.

Certain regions, such as Flanders and northern France, became famous for their fairs. Fairs were held in cycles so that merchants could go from one fair to the next throughout the year. These fairs were held in the same places each year. As the fairs in Flanders and northern France prospered and grew in importance, others disappeared.

In the Byzantine Empire and in Islamic countries, most commerce occurred in the permanent trading centers of large cities. When Muslims went on a pilgrimage to Mecca, the holiest city of Islam, they attended a huge fair that was held after the religious ceremonies. (See also *Agriculture; Trade.*)

Medieval markets were usually located in open, outdoor spaces, where merchants displayed their products. Most of the items for sale were foods, but merchants also sold pottery, spices, and clothing.

Family and Household

Several factors—location, religion, and social class—determined the similarities and differences among families of the Middle Ages. All groups had certain rules and customs about marriage, divorce, family responsibilities, and expectations for their children.

In regions controlled by the Byzantine Empire, most families consisted of a father, a mother, and children. While the father headed the household and managed the money, the mother's main responsibility was raising the children. After the children married or became financially independent, the parents no longer had authority over them.

In the Byzantine world, parents arranged marriages for their children. However, the children also had to agree to the marriage. Beginning at age ten, those who did not want to marry could choose to enter a monastery or a convent. Byzantine laws about divorce were very strict, and the Byzantine Church disapproved of remarriage.

In regions governed by Islamic law, the family was the basic unit of society and was highly valued. Marriage was encouraged for the purpose of producing children. Greater importance was placed on a wife's behavior than on her wealth or beauty. A husband was valued for his kindness to, and support of, his wife.

To promote family unity, Islam set certain rules for married men and women. The husband's role as head of the household required that he support the family. He could have up to four wives, if he could support them. Women were responsible for raising the children, and a good wife was expected to respect and obey her husband. Fathers supported the children until their sons reached maturity or their daughters married. Children were expected to respect and obey their parents.

In Western Europe, family life involved not just fathers, mothers, and children but entire households. A household might include other relatives, servants, and family friends. Western European families varied greatly, depending on social class. In noble families, the lady of the manor was

Medieval Furniture

By today's standards, medieval European households were sparsely furnished. Furniture was expensive, and generally only the wealthy could afford it. Even wealthy homes, however, contained relatively few pieces. Wealthy people often owned more than one home, and they took their furniture with them when they traveled from one home to another. In the event of war or invasion, it was important to have furniture that could be moved quickly.

responsible for running the household. In middle-class families, the wife not only ran the household but also helped her husband with the family business. In peasant society, all family members worked together. Men plowed the fields, built and maintained the home, and made furniture and tools. Women and children worked in the fields and cared for the farm animals.

By the time they were seven, children in Western Europe were considered old enough to receive job training. Children from noble families were often sent to other noble families or to churchmen to learn practical skills. Middle-class children most often learned their fathers' trades or were apprenticed to a merchant or craftsman to learn another trade. Some went to school before their apprenticeship to learn how to read and write. Peasant children generally grew up in their parents' homes, where they began working at an early age.

In Jewish communities, many customs and traditions

Wealthy households often had servants, such as those shown here, attending to the family's needs. This house might have belonged to a Flemish merchant and his family. The first floor would have had a salesroom or workshop. The second floor would have had rooms for the family and for entertaining guests. The bedrooms would have been on the third floor.

favored men over women, and boys over girls. In some regions, Jewish men were allowed to have more than one wife. In general only male children received formal education. In cases of divorce, the laws were less restrictive for men than for women. A women whose husband died was sometimes required to marry one of her husband's brothers. In this way the woman's DOWRY would remain in her husband's family. (See also *Schools and Universities; Women.*)

Feudalism

The term *feudalism* is used to describe the relationship between medieval lords and those who served them. Feudalism occurred at both a local level and a regional level. At the local level, the lord of a castle was the ruler of a particular region. Those who served him were called VASSALS. The vassals pledged their loyalty to the lord and provided him with military and other services. In return, the vassals were given land, which was called a FIEF. Vassals had permission to live on the land and to use it, but they did not own the fief. Vassals used peasants to farm the land, and the peasants paid rent to plant and harvest small sections of it to provide food for their families.

A vassal usually passed a fief on to his heir. But if the vassal was disloyal or did not perform his services to his lord's satisfaction, the fief returned to the lord. Vassals were also expected to provide financial help to their lords. For example, a vassal had to give the lord money for certain expenses, such as ransom payments or special ceremonies.

Just as their vassals owed them loyalty, the local lords were expected to pledge their loyalty to a count, duke, or king. It was generally believed that one's highest loyalty was to the king.

This type of feudalism existed in many parts of Europe. But the level of control exercised by the king over his lords varied from country to country and often led to arguments. In England, for example, the rebellion of the lords against the king's power led to the issuing of Magna Carta. (See also *Magna Carta; Nobles and Knights.*)

A vassal is shown here kneeling before his lord, or king. He pledges his loyalty and service to his lord in return for land.

38

Food and Drink

Buying and selling food and drink was the most common business activity during the Middle Ages.

Securing food for the population was the main concern for many local governments, and the buying and selling of food was the most common business activity in the marketplaces.

During the early Middle Ages, most people grew their own crops and raised animals to feed their families. Food was also used for trade between a lord and the peasants who farmed his land. The lord gave the peasants bread or ale for their work, and the peasants paid their rent with part of the grain they harvested or some of the animals they raised.

By the year 1000, new methods of agriculture were helping farmers produce more and better crops. A larger supply of food led to population growth. Business and trade increased, and by the end of the 1200s, vast new lands had been cleared of forests and were producing grain. This meant that many landowners no longer had to grow their own grain. Instead they could concentrate on other types of agriculture, such as livestock farming, and more foods became available.

People of the Middle Ages ate many of the same foods that are eaten today, although potatoes and corn were eaten only in the Americas. The medieval diet was based on grain, which was used to make bread, buns, and other baked goods. Grain was also used to make porridge, ale, and beer. Fish was eaten often, since Christians were prohibited from eating meat on Fridays and on certain holy days throughout the year. Dairy products—milk, butter, cheese, and eggs—were also popular. Most people grew their own fruits and vegetables.

Wine and ale were the favorite beverages. Nobles, church officials, and wealthy townspeople most often drank wine. Ale—an alcoholic drink made of barley, water, and yeast, with herbs and spices added for flavor—was the most common beverage in northern Europe. Ale spoiled after a few days, so it was brewed frequently by women in their homes. Beer, which is similar to ale, became popular in the late Middle Ages. (See also *Agriculture*.)

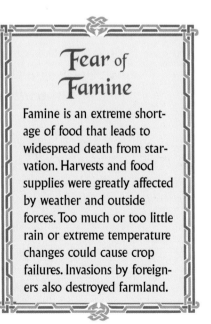

Fear of Famine

Famine is an extreme shortage of food that leads to widespread death from starvation. Harvests and food supplies were greatly affected by weather and outside forces. Too much or too little rain or extreme temperature changes could cause crop failures. Invasions by foreigners also destroyed farmland.

Francis of Assisi

Francis of Assisi, the son of a wealthy cloth merchant, was born in central Italy around 1182. He was popular among his friends and led a happy and carefree life. Francis received little formal education. He learned his father's trade instead of attending a university.

When Francis was in his early 20s, he was captured in battle and held prisoner for a year. Around this time he had a change of heart and decided to alter his way of life. When he returned to Assisi, Francis began to care for the sick and help the poor. Francis's father disapproved of his son's new lifestyle, but Francis was determined.

He organized a group of followers who joined him in living a life of poverty and preaching the GOSPEL. Eventually the group received approval from the pope and became known as the Franciscan order. Francis was a good speaker and attracted many followers. Within two years of his death in 1226, Francis was officially declared a saint. (See also *Clare of Assisi.*)

Frederick Barbarossa

Frederick Barbarossa, lying on the floor, begged the pope to forgive him for breaking the alliance they had formed.

Frederick Barbarossa (Redbeard) was born around 1122. He was elected king of Germany during a time when the country was divided between two powerful families. Frederick was related to both families, and his election helped to prevent a civil war. As king, he then turned his attention to restoring the Holy Roman Empire to its former greatness. He formed an alliance with the pope and was crowned Holy Roman Emperor in 1155.

Frederick soon broke his alliance with the pope and tried to gain control of northern Italy by attacking the region. This move brought Frederick in conflict both with Italian towns and the pope. Eventually, Frederick gave up his plan and arranged a truce with the pope. In 1189, he organized the Third Crusade. But the following year, Frederick drowned while leading his Crusaders across a river.

Genghis Khan, originally named Temüjin, was a conqueror and the founder of the Mongol Empire. Born in 1155, Temüjin was the son of a Mongol chief and ruler. When Temüjin was only nine years old, his father was killed by an enemy tribe. Temüjin was taken prisoner so that he would not seek revenge for his father's death. But he escaped with support from a friend of his father.

Genghis Khan, shown here with his sons, conquered territory that stretched from Eastern Europe to the China Sea.

In the years that followed, Temüjin perfected his military skills and became a powerful leader of the Mongols. Although he was sometimes challenged for this position, Temüjin eventually defeated all of his enemies. In 1206, with the Mongol tribes united behind him, he was proclaimed Genghis Khan, or Universal Ruler.

Under his leadership, the Mongols then began their conquest of China. In 1215 they captured Peking (now called Beijing). Mongol warriors were skilled and ruthless in battle, and they were greatly feared by their enemies. Eventually, Genghis Khan ruled a vast empire that extended from China to Eastern Europe.

Guilds

During the Middle Ages, guilds were groups of merchants or craftspeople who joined together to protect their interests. Guilds contributed to the expansion of trade and to the growth of cities. They developed standards and provided a variety of educational, social, and religious services.

There were two types of guilds: merchant guilds and craft guilds. Merchant guilds were involved in sales and trade. Craft guilds were for skilled workers in particular trades, such as woodworkers, blacksmiths, and bakers. Some guilds admitted women as members.

One important feature of medieval craft guilds was the apprentice system. The members of a craft guild were separated into three classes: apprentice, journeyman, and master. An apprentice was a boy who received training in a craft. He was not paid money for his work, but he was given food and shelter. When an apprentice finished his training, he became a journeyman. A journeyman received payment for his work and could eventually become a master.

Johannes Gutenberg

Johannes Gutenberg—born in Mainz, Germany, around 1400—was a skilled craftsman, inventor, and printer. He is credited with inventing the printing press, which revolutionized the way books were produced. Before Gutenberg's printing press, SCRIBES had to copy each word by hand to make copies of a book. This was very time-consuming and expensive, and therefore most people did not own books, nor did they know how to read.

Around 1450, Gutenberg invented the PRINTING PRESS and a system of arranging metal blocks with raised letters to form words. With these developments, it became possible to mass-produce books. Mass production meant that books became less expensive and more widely available. This development, in turn, encouraged more people to learn how to read and aided the spread of ideas and knowledge.

One of the first books that Gutenberg printed was a Bible that had 42 lines on each page. Twenty perfect copies (and 31 imperfect copies) of this work, known as the Gutenberg Bible, still exist. (See also *Literature.*)

Heloise and Abelard

Heloise, born around 1101, was the niece of a church official in Paris, France. Peter Abelard, born around 1079 in Brittany, France, was a teacher of PHILOSOPHY and THEOLOGY. Abelard became Heloise's teacher, and the two fell in love. Heloise was only 20 years old, and Abelard was about 40. After Heloise had a baby, she and Abelard were secretly married. Their love affair angered Heloise's uncle, and he had Abelard brutally punished.

The tragic love affair of Heloise and Abelard became famous throughout the medieval world.

Abelard then entered a monastery at St. Denis, and Heloise entered a nearby convent. In 1121, Abelard published a work on theology that was condemned by the Church. A year later he built a chapel, which he called Le Paraclet, and a convent. In 1129, Heloise entered that convent, and she and Abelard began exchanging romantic letters.

When Abelard died, around 1142, he was buried at Le Paraclet. When Heloise died years later, she was buried beside her lover. The romance of Heloise and Abelard has inspired writers throughout the centuries. (See also *Monks, Friars, and Nuns.*)

Heraldry

Heraldry is the system of designing and recording the symbols that were used on medieval armor. These symbols were used to identify medieval knights in battle.

Knights fought to defend the castles and lands of the nobility. To protect themselves from their enemies' weapons, knights wore armor and carried shields. They also wore helmets with visors that completely covered their faces, except for their eyes. Even close up, it was impossible to tell one knight from another. In the heat of battle, a knight ran the risk of being injured or killed by a member of his own army. To help warriors recognize one another, they painted symbols on their shields.

Symbols or objects painted on shields enabled knights to recognize each other during a battle.

Knights wore sleeveless coats over their armor to keep the sun from heating up the metal. When identifying emblems were added to these garments, the term *coat of arms* was created.

Those who designed coats of arms followed strict rules. For example, only two colors were used—one dark color and one light color. The dark color was usually blue, red, green, purple, or black. The light color, which represented a precious metal, was either yellow (for gold) or white (for silver). The contrast of the dark and light colors enabled knights to see the coats of arms from great distances.

Officials, known as heralds, kept records of the many coats of arms worn by knights. They used special terms to describe each one accurately. Heralds were especially important during tournaments. The herald was responsible for blazoning—blowing a trumpet when a new knight arrived. Once the herald had the audience's attention, he called out a description of the knight's coat of arms. The word *blazonry* came to mean the detailed description of a coat of arms.

Heresy and the Inquisition

Heresy is a belief that differs from what is generally accepted to be right or true. In the Middle Ages, heresy was any belief that was opposed to the teachings of the Church. Some Christians continued to hold onto their differing beliefs even after the Church questioned those beliefs. Such people were considered HERETICS who should not be allowed in the Church and who deserved to be punished.

Beginning in the 1200s, a person accused of heresy was investigated and tried in a special religious court called an Inquisition. However, few rules existed to ensure that all people accused of heresy were tried and punished in the same way.

Generous rewards were offered for finding heretics. Therefore, people had reason to accuse their neighbors. In addition, those who admitted to being heretics often accused

In this painting, books written by heretics burn, but the Bible, placed in the fire by St. Dominic, floats above the flames undamaged.

others in the hope of receiving a lighter punishment. During an Inquisition, the names of the accusers were kept secret. Anyone who tried to help the accused person, such as a friend or a lawyer, could also be punished.

Some heretics confessed and repented—admitted sinning and said that they felt sorry. These people usually received milder punishments, including fines and being required to go on pilgrimages. When heretics did not repent, they were turned over to nonreligious courts, and their punishments were usually much more severe. These punishments included seizure and destruction of property, long jail terms, banishment, torture, and even death.

The Inquisition remained active for a long time. In the beginning it was used to strengthen the authority of the Church. In Spain, it operated under royal authority and the punishments were harsher.

Holy Roman Empire

The Holy Roman Empire, which grew out of the eastern portion of Charlemagne's realm, dominated the political life of central Europe in the Middle Ages and indeed was important until it ended in 1806. It was viewed as the continuation of the Western Roman Empire. Although its boundaries changed over the years, the German states were always the central region of the empire.

Historians generally date the founding of the Holy Roman Empire to Christmas Day in 800. On that day Pope Leo II crowned Charlemagne "Emperor of the Romans," making him the first medieval ruler to claim succession from the Romans. After Charlemagne's death in 814, his empire fell apart. Then, in 962, Pope John XII made King Otto I "Emperor of the Romans." Otto soon gained control of most of northern and central Italy, defeating the pope's enemies there. Later emperors quarreled with the Church over who had greater power over the empire.

The term *Holy* was introduced later by the supporters of Frederick Barbarossa. They wanted to show that the emperor's power came from God and was independent of the pope. The complete title—Holy Roman Empire—was first used in 1254 and lasted until the end of the empire.

Ibn Battuta

The Muslim writer Ibn Battuta was probably the greatest world traveler of the Middle Ages. His travels may have been more extensive than those of Marco Polo, the famous Italian explorer. Born in 1304 in Tangier, Morocco, in North Africa, he began traveling at the age of 21. His first trip was a pilgrimage to Mecca and Medina, the holy cities of Islam. He enjoyed this journey so much, in fact, that he did not return to Morocco for 24 years. During that time he visited southern Russia, India, China, Spain, and many cities in Africa. He also traveled across the Sahara—the largest desert in the world—to the kingdom of Mali.

When he finally completed his travels, Ibn Battuta settled in North Africa. A Moroccan sultan was so impressed with Ibn Battuta's adventures that he paid a SCRIBE to record them on paper. This work is called the *Rihla,* which means "travels." In it Ibn Battuta describes the people, places, and events of his many exciting journeys. This record provides important geographical and historical information about the medieval world.

Ibn Rushd

Ibn Rushd, also known as Averroës, was a philosopher and physician in Muslim Spain. He was born in the city of Córdoba in 1126. A great scholar, Ibn Rushd studied PHILOSOPHY, THEOLOGY, mathematics, and medicine. His father, who was a judge, taught him about Muslim law.

Ibn Rushd had studied the works of the ancient Greek philosopher Aristotle. At the request of the caliph, the Muslim ruler in Spain, Ibn Rushd wrote essays about the works of Aristotle. He tried to find a way to blend the views of philosophy and religion. He believed that it was necessary to study philosophy in order to prove the existence of God. Ibn Rushd also wrote books on Islamic law, medicine, and ASTRONOMY and became the chief physician of the ruler of Spain.

Problems occurred, however, when the caliph disagreed with some of Ibn Rushd's opinions. In 1195 the caliph banished him from Spain and burned his books. Ibn Rushd later returned as chief physician of the royal court, but he died soon thereafter. His influence over both Muslim and Christian scholars lasted well into the RENAISSANCE, many years after his death.

Ibn Rushd, shown here, taught that the study of philosophy can lead to proof of God's existence.

Ibn Sina

Born in Persia in 980, Ibn Sina—also known as Avicenna—was an Islamic scholar, poet, and physician. He was a respected physician by age 16, and he went on to serve as court physician or government official for several Persian rulers. In addition, he worked as a scientific adviser and a teacher.

Ibn Sina's greatest lasting achievements were his writings. He wrote more than 200 works on such varied subjects as medicine, PHILOSOPHY, politics, sociology, and grammar. For many years his medical book *The Canon of Medicine* was the leading textbook in the Middle East and Europe. Translated into Latin, Hebrew, and Arabic, it is perhaps the most famous medical book ever written. Ibn Sina's best-known philosophy work is *The Book of Healing.* It is organized in four sections: LOGIC, philosophy, mathematics, and METAPHYSICS. This work was the largest encyclopedia of knowledge created by a single person in the Middle Ages.

46

Icons

Icons are paintings of Jesus Christ, the Virgin Mary, and the saints. These paintings are especially important in the Eastern Christian Church. To Eastern Christians, icons are sacred objects, and they are displayed in homes, churches, and monasteries. The faithful show their devotion by praying and lighting candles and incense in front of these icons.

During the Middle Ages, those who painted icons were expected to follow specific rules. Portraits were usually painted as half-length or full-length figures viewed from the front. The people in these paintings sometimes look unreal. The painter tried to highlight the spiritual nature of these holy figures rather than their human qualities.

People disagreed about the use of icons. Most early Christians were against the use of religious images. They felt that icons were a form of idolatry—the worship of a physical object as a god.

During the 700s, the disagreement over icons reached a peak among Eastern Christians. In 726, Byzantine emperor Leo III adopted a policy of iconoclasm—the removal or destruction of icons in churches. The next emperor, Constantine V, also enforced this policy. But in 787, at a church council in Nicaea, the Byzantine empress Irene declared that icons should be restored. The iconoclastic movement did not end completely, however, until 842. From then on, icons became an important part of Eastern Orthodox Christianity and an important feature of Byzantine art. (See also *Art; Byzantine Empire; Christianity.*)

This icon shows the Virgin Mary holding Jesus. On either side of Mary stands a saint; behind her are two angels.

Inca Empire

The Inca Empire was the largest American Indian civilization that ever existed. Originally a small tribe living in the Andean highlands, the Inca built an empire in South America that included parts of present-day Ecuador, Peru, Bolivia, Chile, and Argentina. By the mid-1400s, this vast region was linked by hundreds of miles of roads and ruled by an emperor.

Inca life was devoted to supporting the empire. Most people were required to pay taxes by giving the government part of their crops and by helping to build roads and bridges. Storehouses alongside the roads were filled with food, clothes, and weapons for the messengers who traveled on foot to deliver news to the emperor and receive commands to take back to the workers. Instead of a written language, the Inca used quipu—a system of knotted strings of different colors and lengths—to keep track of tax payments and storehouse supplies.

Religion was a major part of Inca life. The people worshiped the emperor as a living god. When he died, they mummified his body to preserve it. The most sacred shrine was the Temple of the Sun, where animals and sometimes humans were sacrificed to ensure an abundant harvest. Inca priests developed a calendar by observing the movements of the sun and moon. They also served as doctors and were skilled at amputating arms and legs and preventing infections.

After Emperor Huayna Capac died in 1525, the empire was severely weakened. His two sons fought with each other to decide who would replace him. Soon after the fighting ended, the Spanish explorer Francisco Pizarro invaded the empire with 150 men. Armed with guns, which the Inca did not have, the Spaniards captured Atahualpa, the new emperor. Pizarro demanded a room filled with gold and two rooms filled with silver as ransom. Although his demands were met, he still executed the emperor and destroyed the empire.

The Inca heritage survived the death of its last emperor. Quechua, the language of the Inca, is still spoken by millions of Indians in South America.

Machu Picchu, the site of the ruins of the Inca royal estate, is located high in the Andes mountains of Peru.

Inns and Taverns

Because many people were unable to read, innkeepers often placed pitchers or plates in their windows so that travelers would know that they could buy food and drink there.

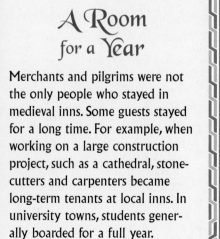

Medieval travelers, like modern ones, needed places where they could eat and rest after a long day on the road. In the early Middle Ages, a traveler could often spend the night free of charge in a private home or a monastery. Most households and monasteries felt that it was their responsibility to provide food and lodging to weary travelers. Pilgrims on their way to the Holy Land were welcome to spend the night at hospitals as well.

In the early 1100s, as more merchants began to travel the roads, the lodging situation changed. Free hospitality became more difficult to find. In some European countries, inns and others types of lodging—both commercial and private—could be found all along a traveler's route. Inns on well-traveled roads prospered.

Many inns were actually ordinary houses that were furnished for guests. These buildings typically had three types of rooms: a kitchen, a main hall, and bedrooms. Several beds were usually found in each bedroom, and several people often slept in each bed. Innkeepers used various methods to advertise their business. Some owners put objects such as plates and pitchers in their windows; others placed signs on their front doors.

Medieval taverns were simple structures where people gathered to eat and drink, conduct business, or just enjoy the company of others. Taverns were common meeting places for merchants and students in particular. Although not everyone approved of taverns, they remained popular throughout the Middle Ages.

A Room for a Year

Merchants and pilgrims were not the only people who stayed in medieval inns. Some guests stayed for a long time. For example, when working on a large construction project, such as a cathedral, stonecutters and carpenters became long-term tenants at local inns. In university towns, students generally boarded for a full year.

Islam

Islam, one of the world's major religions, is practiced by millions of people throughout the world. The term *Islam* is Arabic for "submission." The people of Islam, called Muslims, believe in one god, Allah. They follow the practices and teachings of Muhammad, the PROPHET and founder of Islam. During the Middle Ages, Islam spread from the Middle East into southern Asia, North Africa, and Europe, uniting many people under a single religion.

The Muslim Book of Sacred Writings

The Qur'an, also spelled "Koran," contains the holy writings of Islam. The word *qur'an* means "recitation." The writings in this book are memorized by Muslims and recited during their daily prayers.

The Qur'an is written in Arabic and contains 114 chapters called suras. The suras vary in length from a few lines to several hundred lines. The Qur'an is the supreme authority on all matters of Islamic law and religion.

Before the rise of Islam, the people of the Arabian peninsula worshiped several gods. In the early 600s, however, Muhammad began preaching about Allah. Muhammad's preachings were based on divine messages, called revelations, which he believed he had received from Allah commanding him to spread God's word. The Qur'an—the holy book of Islam—is the collection of these divine revelations. In time, and with armed followers, Muhammad brought much of Arabia under Islam.

The basic religious duties of all Muslims are known as the Five Pillars of Faith. The first is the *shahada*—the statement of faith and belief in Allah and his prophet Muhammad. The second pillar is the *salat*—the prayer that is recited five times each day while facing in the direction of Mecca, Islam's holiest city. The third pillar is *zakat*—the giving of money or gifts to the needy. The fourth pillar is *sawm,* or fasting during Ramadan, a period when Muslims do not eat or drink between dawn and dusk. The fifth pillar is the hajj—a pilgrimage to the holy city of Mecca. All able Muslims are required to make at least one hajj in their lifetimes.

After Muhammad died in 632, his followers began a series of military conquests with the intent of spreading the Islamic religion. With the first conquests, Islamic armies captured much of the Middle East, including Arabia, Egypt, Syria, and Iraq. They went on to conquer Iran, Afghanistan, and the Indus River valley in India. In later conquests, Muslims seized North Africa and parts of Spain. These conquests resulted in a vast new empire that dominated much of the medieval world.

The most important Islamic buildings are mosques, Muslim places of worship. The mosque that Muhammad established was a simple open structure. As time passed, however, mosques became larger and more ornate. The basic elements of a mosque include a courtyard where worshipers pray, tall slender towers called minarets, and a small space—called a mihrab—which marks the spot where Muhammad stood while leading his followers in prayers. During prayer, worshipers face the mihrab.

By the end of the Middle Ages, Muslims had come into contact with the art and architecture of other regions. They combined these cultural elements with their own to create an artistic style that was both distinctive and diverse, reflecting each region of the Islamic world. (See also *Science and Technology.*)

The Dome of the Rock in Jerusalem marks the place where Muhammad is said to have ascended to heaven.

Jerusalem

Jerusalem is a holy city for Jews, Christians, and Muslims. The most important city in Palestine, Jerusalem had been a center of Judaism for 3,000 years before the Middle Ages began. During the Middle Ages, Jews made pilgrimages to Jerusalem. They went to visit the ruins of the Second Temple, which had been destroyed by the Romans in A.D. 70.

For Christians, Jerusalem is important as the place where Jesus Christ was CRUCIFIED and buried and then rose from the dead. Religious monuments were built in Jerusalem to celebrate the life of Christ. One of the most important monuments for Christians was the Church of the Holy Sepulcher, which was built on the site of Christ's tomb. As Christians began to make pilgrimages to Jerusalem, inns and other accommodations were built for their convenience.

To Muslims, Jerusalem is the third holiest city, after Mecca and Medina. Mecca is the birthplace of Muhammad, the prophet and founder of Islam. Medina is the city he fled to when his safety was threatened. But Jerusalem is also important to Muslims because several significant events in Muhammad's life occurred there. Muslims built several monuments in the city. One such monument is the Dome of the Rock, built on the site where Muslims believe Muhammad rose to heaven.

In 1099, during the First Crusade, Christians captured Jerusalem from the Muslims. A Christian king was installed there, making Jerusalem a royal capital. The Crusaders tore down many old buildings and constructed new ones. They also tried to convert the city's inhabitants to Christianity.

In 1187, the Muslim military leader and VIZIER Saladin recaptured Jerusalem. In the 1200s the city returned by treaty to Christian hands. But in 1244 it was captured by Muslims once again, and it remained in Muslim hands for the rest of the Middle Ages. (See also *Crusades; Muhammad; Pilgrimage.*)

This painting shows the capture of Jerusalem during the First Crusade. At the right, Crusaders are shown killing the Muslims and Jews of the city.

Judaism is an ancient religion. People who practice Judaism are called Jews. In the A.D. 100s, the Romans banished the Jews from Palestine. Because they were not allowed to return to their homeland, Jews began to spread out into new lands. During the Middle Ages, Jewish communities developed throughout Europe and the Islamic world. But the Jews were at the mercy of the leaders and people of their new homelands. In some regions, Jewish communities became major cultural centers. In other places, they did not fare so well.

Jews followed a strict set of religious beliefs, practices, and laws. They resisted pressures to convert to other religions and would not marry outside of their faith. These attitudes were often a source of conflict between Jews and their neighbors of other religions. Because the Jews were in many places denied the right to own property, they kept their wealth in money or precious stones. In addition, the Catholic Church barred believers from lending money, so many Jews became moneylenders, which was among the few occupations open to them.

This painting shows members of a Jewish community preparing to celebrate Passover—a holiday commemorating the Jews' liberation from slavery in Pharaoh's Egypt.

Despite these problems, Jewish communities thrived in some parts of Europe, including Spain, Italy, and France, in the early Middle Ages. In these countries, many rulers respected Jews and supported their religious rights and activities. The Jews became an important minority and were considered a valuable part of society. In the later Middle Ages, however, hostility toward Jews began to increase. One reason may have been the deep devotion of Jews to their religion, which was seen as a threat to the Christian church. Such attitudes led to Jews being expelled, or banished, from several European countries. (See also *Heresy and the Inquisition.*)

Joan of Arc

Joan of Arc was born in France in 1412. At that time the Hundred Years' War was being fought between England and France, and the English occupied part of France. When she was only 13, Joan heard the voices of saints telling her to save France and help Charles, the eldest son of the king of France, become king. Later, after convincing Charles and the Church that her mission was real, Joan was allowed to join the battle. Dressed in armor, she led French troops to an important victory over the English. Charles was later crowned king of France.

Joan continued to fight and was captured by the enemy. Because she wore men's clothing, behaved like a soldier (which was unusual for a girl), and insisted that saints had spoken to her, she was accused of HERESY. Dressed in women's clothes at her trial, Joan was found guilty and sentenced to life in prison. But when she continued to wear men's clothing in jail, she was condemned to death. In 1431, Joan of Arc was burned at the stake. Many people mourned her death, and the pope canceled her sentence in 1456. More than 500 years after her death, the church made her a saint.

Accused of heresy and witchcraft, Joan of Arc was burned at the stake.

Kublai Khan

Born around 1216, Kublai Khan was the grandson and a successor of Genghis Khan, the Mongol conqueror. Genghis Khan had begun the conquest of China that Kublai Khan completed years later. At first, Kublai was helping his brother Mangu, the fourth great-khan, conquer southern China. But when Mangu Khan died, Kublai became the khan—ruler of the Mongol Empire.

In 1264, Kublai Khan established his capital at Khanbalik (present-day Beijing). There he became the founder and first emperor of the Yuan DYNASTY, which ruled China for more than a century. During his reign, Kublai Khan encouraged the growth of literature and the arts and established cultural relations with other countries. He made Buddhism the state religion of China. Kublai Khan was interested in many things and welcomed visitors to his court. His most famous visitor was Marco Polo.

Law

The laws governing societies during the Middle Ages varied greatly from place to place and from culture to culture. The Roman Empire's surviving territories, known as the Byzantine Empire, preserved Roman law. In the 500s, Byzantine emperor Justinian I organized Roman laws into a collection. Much later, the collection became the basis of study at law schools in Italy and spread throughout Europe.

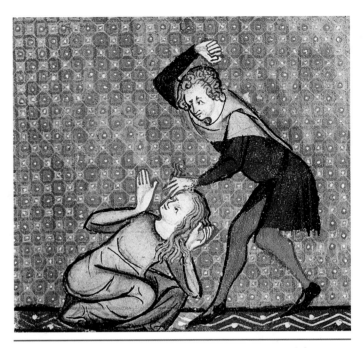

In some places, a man was not even punished for beating his wife, unless he was drunk or in a bad temper when he beat her.

Most Roman laws fell into disuse in Western Europe after the fall of the Roman Empire. The Germanic tribes that had conquered the empire had their own laws and traditions, but they were unwritten. Therefore, two people found guilty of the same crime might be punished differently. In addition, separate laws existed for three classes of Germanic society—slaves, former slaves, and free citizens.

The religious laws of the Roman Catholic Church, known as canon law, provided the only legal unity in Western Europe. Canon law was based in part on Roman law. Because almost everyone in Western Europe was Christian, canon law affected most of the population.

Islamic law, known as shari'a, is based on the Qur'an (the holy book of Islam) and governs the everyday life of all Muslims. Muslims believe that Islamic law came from God; therefore, it is universal. Islam teaches that all Muslims are equal in the eyes of God and that Islamic law applies to all Muslims, regardless of class.

Jewish law comes from Jewish tradition and the first five books of the Bible, which are known as the Torah. Jewish law helped to unify the Jewish communities that were scattered throughout Europe and the Islamic world. Because of their strong traditions, Jews were allowed to govern themselves by their own laws in many places. Some Jewish communities even had their own jails. The most serious form of Jewish punishment was to be banned from participating in the community's religious and cultural life. (See also *Ordeals*.)

Literature

Some of the world's greatest literature was written during the Middle Ages. Medieval literature includes stories, poems, epics, sagas, romances, and religious writings.

The first major poem to be written in the English language was *Beowulf.* The unknown author may have lived as early as the 600s or 700s. Set in Scandinavia, this 3,000-line poem describes the battles of a young warrior named Beowulf. In the poem, Beowulf mortally wounds the monster Grendel, who has been killing and eating the king's warriors. The young hero later kills Grendel's mother and a fire-breathing dragon.

The late 1300s are generally considered the first golden age of English literature. The best-known author of this period was Geoffrey Chaucer, whose masterpiece was *Canterbury Tales,* a collection of stories about a group of travelers who are making a pilgrimage.

In Iceland and other parts of Scandinavia, long adventure stories, or sagas, were written down in the 1200s in the Old Norse language. These sagas described Viking raids, great feuds, and even the Norse discovery of America, which the Vikings called Vinland.

One of the most famous works of French literature is *The Song of Roland.* This epic poem, written around 1100, describes the noble deeds of the emperor Charlemagne and his nephew Roland. Around this time, a new type of literature—the romance—developed in France. The medieval romance combined literary learning and the theme of courtly love. One famous example was the *Romance of the Rose,* which has two parts. The first part tells about a man entering a beautiful garden and falling in love with a rose. A second author continued the poem, with the lover still trying to win the rose, but this author also included his own views on the issues of his time.

In the late Middle Ages, narrative romances were a popular form of literature. Wolfram von Eschenbach was one of Germany's greatest writers during that time. His famous romance, *Parzival,* is about a young knight who has many adventures serving King Arthur.

In Spain, too, medieval poets composed epics about heroic deeds and historical events. The longest and best-known Spanish epic is *Poema de mío Cid.* Written around 1207, this poem describes

Troublemaker or Hero?

Stories about Robin Hood probably began in the 1300s. Little is known about the real Robin Hood. He may have been an outlaw who lived in the woods. As minstrels sang about his adventures, he was transformed into the hero who stole from the rich to help the poor. Whoever he was, he has remained a popular figure in books and movies.

the real-life adventures of a Spanish hero who was called El Cid (from the Arabic word meaning "lord").

During most of the medieval period, Hebrew literature consisted mostly of religious writings. Then, in the late Middle Ages, Jewish poets began to write nonreligious, or secular, works. This later Hebrew poetry often combined Italian and Arabic influences into a distinctive new style.

Medieval Italian poetry was some of the finest literature ever created. Dante Alighieri and Francesco Petrarca (known in English as Petrarch) are considered Italy's greatest poets. When Dante wrote the *Divine Comedy,* he included his political views in the work. He put all of his enemies in Hell and all of his friends in Heaven. Petrarch, who lived in the 1300s, wrote a collection of

This illustration is from a famous story about two doomed lovers—Tristan and Iseult. One of the most popular love stories ever, the tragic tale of Tristan and Iseult has been the subject of many poems and an opera.

poems, the *Rime,* which he dedicated to Laura, a beautiful French woman whom he loved. Petrarch is probably best known for the hundreds of letters he wrote to people throughout Europe. These letters provide a rich view of late medieval life.

Arabic poetry goes back to pre-Islamic times, when poems were recited by professional singers to the NOMADIC tribes in the desert. The most famous work of medieval Arabic literature in the West is the *Thousand and One Nights.* This collection of stories includes fairy tales, romances, fables, legends, and poems. The stories come from many people and places. The earliest manuscript fragments date back to the 800s. The first complete text of this work did not appear until the 1400s. (See also *Gutenberg, Johannes; Manuscripts and Books.*)

Throughout human history, people have sought to understand the differences between the natural and supernatural worlds. To Western Europeans of the Middle Ages, events were either natural or unnatural. *Natural* referred to the usual, ordinary events that occurred in nature. *Unnatural* referred to events that were out of the ordinary—things that were remarkable or unknown. Magic involved creating unnatural events that seemed to defy the laws of nature. There were two types of magic—white magic and black magic. White magic involved entertaining tricks, household formulas, and medications. Black magic, which was also called sorcery, was believed to involve evil forces, such as the devil or other demons.

This painting shows an alchemist at work. Alchemists used a combination of magic and chemistry to attempt to change lead and copper into more valuable metals such as gold and silver.

Medieval people placed great value on symbols that represented objects in nature. Animals, plants, and numbers were commonly used as symbols. The lion represented Jesus Christ. The number seven was thought to have special importance. It represented

the seven known planets and the seven basic colors in nature. The color red represented Mars and was a symbol of success and kindness. Green, which was linked to Venus, meant hope.

Folk magic included the use of charms, spells, and amulets—small objects that are worn as magic charms and are believed to keep away evil. Despite the Church's disapproval of magic, magicians who could cast spells were extremely popular. Foretelling the future, an idea that came from the ancient practice of divination, was a strong tradition in the Byzantine world. Interest in astrology—the study of the influence of the stars and planets on human nature—was also strong. In fact, medieval scholars collected astrological writings from ancient times into encyclopedias.

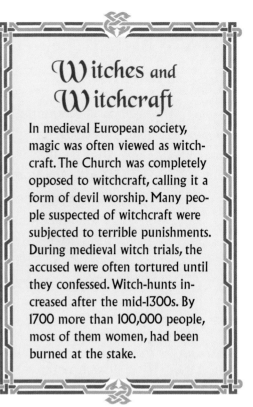

Witches and Witchcraft

In medieval European society, magic was often viewed as witchcraft. The Church was completely opposed to witchcraft, calling it a form of devil worship. Many people suspected of witchcraft were subjected to terrible punishments. During medieval witch trials, the accused were often tortured until they confessed. Witch-hunts increased after the mid-1300s. By 1700 more than 100,000 people, most of them women, had been burned at the stake.

The stories and traditions that people pass down to their children and grandchildren are known as folklore. Magic and folklore are described in the Talmud—the book of Jewish religious law and tradition. Some parts of the Talmud discuss magic, legends, myths, astrology, and amulets. Folktales and stories of the supernatural and those involving evil spirits, demons, and witches were also included in one of the most popular works of Judaism—a book called *Sefer Hasidim.* Written in medieval Germany, the *Sefer Hasidim* describes how people could defend themselves against evil spirits.

Much of Islamic magic and folklore involves jinn, invisible spirits that lived in trees, rocks, caves, and even in people. Jinn (from which the word *genie* comes) were the Arabic equivalent of the fairies, nymphs, and satyrs found in the folklore of Europe. Muhammad, the prophet and founder of Islam, believed that jinn existed. He allowed the use of magical spells to help with some problems, such as in treating certain diseases and as a remedy for poison. Officially, however, magic was frowned upon. According to the Qur'an, the holy book of Islam, magic is harmful. Medieval Muslim leaders, however, distinguished between true (officially approved) magic and false (officially unapproved) magic. Jinn, giants, and vampirelike creatures appear in the *Thousand and One Nights,* a collection of stories that is still read and enjoyed by many. (See also *Medicine.*)

Magna Carta

Magna Carta, which means Great Charter, is one of the most famous documents in English history. In the early 1200s, a group of English nobles were unhappy with the way King John was governing the country. Under the leadership of a churchman named Stephen Langton, they created the charter as a means of guaranteeing their rights. The nobles forced King John to seal Magna Carta in 1215 at Runnymede, southwest of London. By approving this document, the king acknowledged that he had to obey the law just like everyone else. The charter also limited the king's power over his subjects.

Magna Carta contains 63 articles, covering many aspects of medieval life. The articles can be grouped into five main areas: the rights of the church, royal courts, financial matters, the treasury, and the sharing of power between the king and his nobles.

Although the noble classes benefited most from Magna Carta, the charter's protections were eventually granted to all English people. This document was an important stepping-stone in the development of constitutional government in England and other countries, including the United States and Canada. (See also *Seals and Signets.*)

Maimonides

Moses ben Maimon, known as Maimonides, was a Jewish PHILOSOPHER, THEOLOGIAN, and physician. He was born in Córdoba, Spain, in 1135. His family decided to leave the city when it was captured by the Almohads, who were forcing Jews and Christians to become Muslims. After many years of wandering, Maimonides eventually settled in Cairo, Egypt. There he became the chief rabbi—leader of the Jewish community. He also became a chief physician for Saladin, a Muslim military leader and VIZIER.

Maimonides wrote several important works, including books on philosophy, ASTRONOMY, medicine, and LOGIC. The work for which he is best known, however, is about Jewish law and religious beliefs. The *Mishneh Torah* (Summary of the Law) is a 14-volume work that organizes and explains Jewish law. This work was completed around 1178 and influenced several Christian philosophers, including Thomas Aquinas. The *Mishneh Torah* is such an important work that it is still read, studied, and discussed by students and theologians.

Maimonides died in 1204 in Cairo, Egypt. In accordance with his wishes, he was buried in Tiberias (in present-day Israel). (See also *Ibn Rushd; Ibn Sina; Jewish Communities.*)

Manuscripts and Books

Before the late Middle Ages, books were written by hand. They were called manuscripts, from Latin words meaning "written by hand." Because manuscripts were created one at a time, each was unique. Many contained not only words but also illustrations called illuminations. Some manuscripts were so beautifully illustrated and carefully crafted that they were considered works of art.

Producing a book was a complicated process. First, sheets of PARCH-MENT had to be smoothed and cut to size. Each sheet was folded in half so that it became two facing pages. The pages were numbered and marked with ruled lines. Using these lines as guides, SCRIBES copied the text by hand onto the paper with black ink. Scribes used pens made of QUILLS or REEDS.

Based on a medieval ivory carving, this illustration shows Gregory, a monk who became pope, at work. He is inspired in his writing by the Holy Spirit, shown as a dove on his shoulder.

Printing in China

In the 800s, the Chinese had invented wood-block printing. In this method, characters were drawn on paper, which was pressed upside down on a woodblock, leaving a stain. The wood around the stain was cut away, producing raised letters, on which ink was applied. A clean sheet of paper was pressed onto the inked characters to produce a print.

When the manuscript was finished, the pages were stitched together and attached to a book cover. A variety of materials—such as leather, cloth, wood, and parchment—were used to make book covers. Some book covers were adorned with semiprecious and precious stones.

In about 1450, book production changed forever when a German printer named Johannes Gutenberg invented the PRINTING PRESS. This invention meant that books no longer had to be copied by hand but instead could be mass-produced. Because the printing press allowed books to be produced much more quickly and inexpensively, books became available to a greater number of people (See also *Literature*.)

Maps and Mapmaking

The quality of any map is only as good as the mapmaker's knowledge of the area to be charted, or mapped. Based on the limited information available about the regions of the world, ancient maps reflected the popular beliefs of the time. Medieval geography—the study of the earth's surface—combined science, literature, and art. The written records of traders, explorers, and geographers of the Middle Ages made possible the centuries of exploration and discovery that followed.

During the early Middle Ages, the *mappa mundi* was the main type of world map used in Western Europe. This circular map showed Europe and those parts of Asia and Africa that were known at the time. Because these maps reflected Christian beliefs, the holy city of Jerusalem was located at the top of the map. The maps were often decorated with drawings of legendary figures or special places.

The invention of the compass—probably in the 1100s—revolutionized medieval mapmaking. Because north was at the top of the compass, mapmakers began to put north at the tops of maps. The development of two other tools—the astrolabe and the quadrant—also changed mapmaking. The astrolabe was used for determining the position of the stars, for telling time, and for navigating. The quadrant was used to measure altitude. These instruments helped to make navigation more precise, thus improving the accuracy of mapmaking.

Using their new navigational tools, sailors made many important discoveries. Explorers and traders ventured into new lands and returned with information about these regions. Maps were changing as new information was discovered and recorded.

In the Islamic world, two different methods of mapmaking developed during the 900s and 1000s. In one, Iraq was centrally located in the Islamic empire. In the other, the holy city of Mecca was placed at the center. Followers of the second method presented the idea of countries as geographic units. They also considered the races, religions, languages, customs, and occupations of the people who lived in a particular region.

Early mapmaking, or cartography, required exceptional drawing skill, and many cartographers

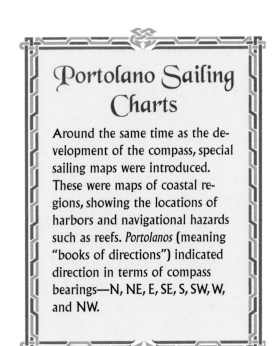

Portolano Sailing Charts

Around the same time as the development of the compass, special sailing maps were introduced. These were maps of coastal regions, showing the locations of harbors and navigational hazards such as reefs. *Portolanos* (meaning "books of directions") indicated direction in terms of compass bearings—N, NE, E, SE, S, SW, W, and NW.

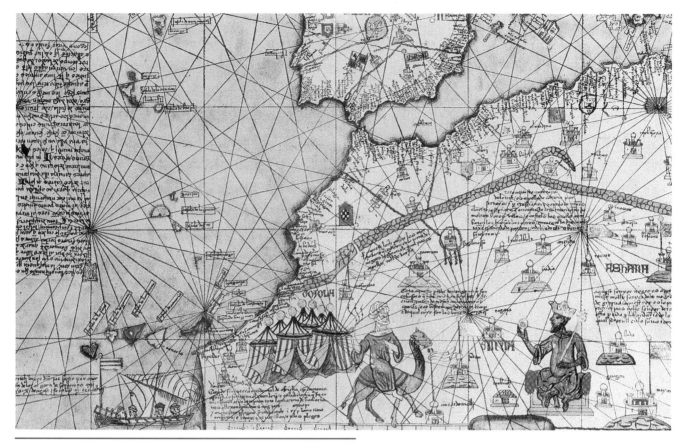

Medieval maps were often decorated with drawings of legendary figures or special places.

began as artists. Because maps were made by hand, each was different, if only slightly. With the invention of the PRINTING PRESS, many copies of the same map could be produced. Even so, many sailors preferred the hand-drawn maps, which they considered more accurate. Some medieval maps have survived to modern times. The Hereford map, made around 1280, is in Hereford Cathedral in England. The Ebstorf map, made in 1284, was discovered in the 1800s in a monastery in Germany, but it was destroyed during World War II. Both maps may have served as church decorations. Historians believe that they were used to show how far Christianity had spread throughout the world.

Medieval road maps were similar to modern travel guides. They were especially useful to people who made pilgrimages to the holy cities and SHRINES. These maps did not show scale or location. However, they provided detailed information about the distances between points along a route and about the features (such as mountains or rivers) and accommodations (such as inns and churches) that a traveler could expect to encounter on the journey. (See also *Ibn Battuta; Science and Technology.*)

63

Marco Polo

The Italian explorer Marco Polo was born in Venice in 1254. His father and uncle were traders, and in 1271 they planned a trip to Asia and took young Marco with them. They traveled for four years before reaching Xanadu, the summer palace of the Mongol emperor Kublai Khan. The Polos were among the first Europeans to travel to Asia. Kublai Khan was so impressed with Marco Polo that he offered him a job. The young man's mission as an inspector for the great-khan took him to China and Southeast Asia. While he was in the royal capital, Marco Polo carefully observed the customs of the khan's court. In 1292, Kublai Khan ordered Marco Polo to escort a Mongol princess to Persia, where she was to marry the khan's great-nephew.

After 24 years away from home, Marco Polo returned to Venice in 1295, but his adventures were far from over. He took part in a sea battle between Venice and Genoa, a rival Italian trading city, and was captured. While in prison, he dictated *The Travels of Marco Polo* to a fellow prisoner. The book provided vivid details about the people and places he had encountered in the East. To most Europeans, this information was new and fascinating. It even inspired Christopher Columbus's interest in Asia, which led to his exploration of America in 1492. (See also *Trade; Transportation.*)

Matilda of Tuscany

Matilda of Tuscany, born in 1046, was an Italian countess who became the ruler of much of northern Italy. She was a central figure in the Investiture Controversy—a major disagreement between Holy Roman Emperor Henry IV and Pope Gregory VII concerning the right to appoint bishops.

For many years, the Holy Roman emperors had wanted the rights to the vast landholdings that Matilda had inherited from her parents. Having this land would have increased their power in Italy. But after Matilda married a relative of the pope, she sided with the popes in their conflict with the emperors. After her husband died, Matilda promised to leave her lands to the office of the pope. This move greatly angered the emperor, and he removed some of Matilda's titles. But when a new emperor came to power, Matilda made peace with him. She changed her mind and decided to leave her lands to the emperor instead of to the pope. Matilda's lands continued to cause problems between emperors and popes for more than a century. (See also *Christianity.*)

Mecca

The western Arabian city of Mecca was the birthplace of Muhammad, the prophet and founder of Islam. For this reason, Mecca is the holiest city in Islam and the most common pilgrimage destination for Muslims. A pilgrimage to Mecca is called a hajj, and faithful Muslims are required to make this journey once during their lifetimes. In addition, no matter where in the world they live, Muslims face Mecca during their daily prayers.

Before the rise of Islam, the people of Mecca believed in more than one god. At that time Meccans worshiped at the great monument called the Kaaba. This cube-shaped SHRINE contained sacred relics. The most sacred of these is the Black Stone. The Kaaba became the holiest shrine in Islam, as it still is.

In the years before Islam, Mecca was an international center of trade and culture. After the spread of Islam, beginning in the 600s, the city continued to thrive as Muslim pilgrims journeyed there from great distances. While in Mecca, the pilgrims had opportunities to trade goods, share ideas, and study Islamic religion and culture. For about 300 years the religious and political leaders of Islam—known as caliphs—encouraged the city's growth. They also appointed princes to run the city.

Muslims are shown here visiting the Kaaba, Islam's holiest shrine. According to Muslim tradition, the Kaaba contains the Black Stone, which was given to Abraham by the angel Gabriel.

By the end of the 900s, however, the caliphs no longer controlled Mecca. The city government had been transferred to the local princes, who were no longer under the influence of the caliphs. In the 1200s, Mecca came under Egyptian rule. In the 1500s the city came under Ottoman rule. Nevertheless, Mecca never lost its importance as the most sacred city of Islam. (See also *Constantinople; Jerusalem.*)

Medicine

Medical knowledge during the Middle Ages was based largely on ancient Greek and Roman ideas. The Byzantine Empire and the Islamic world had preserved and translated the writings of ancient Greek philosophers and physicians, such as Hippocrates, Aristotle, and Galen. Western Europeans did not have access to these works until the 1000s. Because of this, medicine was more advanced in Byzantine and Islamic regions than in Western Europe during the Middle Ages.

The Byzantine Empire made several important contributions to medicine. Aetios of Amida, who lived in the 500s, was one of the first important Christian physicians. He wrote detailed descriptions of diseases, poisons, and infections. Around the same time, another Byzantine doctor, Alexander of Tralles, wrote a medical textbook that was used throughout the Middle

A physician is shown here consulting a medical book for advice on how to treat his injured patient.

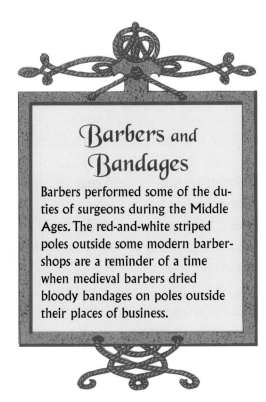

Barbers and Bandages

Barbers performed some of the duties of surgeons during the Middle Ages. The red-and-white striped poles outside some modern barbershops are a reminder of a time when medieval barbers dried bloody bandages on poles outside their places of business.

Ages. Other Byzantine medical scholars collected information about diseases and drugs in reference books for use by doctors. The empire had medical schools and hospitals where both men and women studied and practiced medicine.

Some of the greatest contributions to medical knowledge during the Middle Ages came from the Islamic world. Al-Razi, a physician born in Persia (present-day Iran), discovered the difference between smallpox and measles. Ibn Sina, known as the Prince of Physicians, wrote a medical encyclopedia called *The Canon of Medicine*. Written in the early 1000s, it contained much of the medical knowledge of the time. Maimonides, a Jewish doctor who lived within the Islamic world, wrote on HYGIENE and greatly influenced medicine during the Middle Ages.

Muslims also built hospitals, including one in Damascus and one in Cairo. The Cairo hospital was the first to have separate wards for specific diseases and a large collection of medical textbooks in its library.

Medicine in Western Europe was far less advanced. Physicians could check a patient's pulse and observe symptoms of disease. Medicine and religion were closely associated, and disease was often thought of as a spiritual ailment. Many physicians were monks who were expected to hear a patient's confessions before starting treatment. Christians considered it a religious duty to care for the sick, and this view led to the building of many hospitals.

In the 900s a medical school was established in Salerno, Italy. By the 1000s it had become a major center of medical learning, and it influenced the study and practice of medicine throughout Europe. Students relied on the writings of ancient physicians for knowledge, but they also learned by observing experienced doctors.

However, all the medical knowledge acquired during the Middle Ages was useless when the Black Death struck. This terrible plague first appeared in Europe in 1347. It was caused by bacteria that were spread to humans by the fleas living on infected rats. The origin of the plague was unknown during the Middle Ages, although there were many theories. Physicians in Paris claimed that the alignment of three planets had caused poisonous fumes to invade the earth and kill the people.

Mills Dikes

Throughout history, water has been the most important natural resource. It is essential for the growth and survival of human beings, animals, and crops. During the Middle Ages, people learned how to use the enormous power of moving water to do work.

Water mills are machines that use waterpower to perform various tasks. Although they had been used since ancient Roman times, technological improvements during the Middle Ages increased their usefulness. Most medieval water mills had a large paddle wheel that was turned by moving water. The many swiftly running rivers in Europe made it an ideal place for water mills, and thousands were built. Because water mills were expensive to build and operate, only the wealthy could afford to do so. Owners recovered the money they spent on building the water mill by making peasants pay to use the mill, usually with food or labor.

During the Middle Ages, people also learned to control the destructive powers of water. Uncontrolled floodwaters can ruin crops, destroy homes, and kill people and animals. In the Netherlands, along the North Sea, much of the land is below sea level. The threat of flooding was almost constant. The people who lived there, the Dutch, needed a way to drain the water so that they could use the land.

To accomplish this, they constructed dikes—banks of earth and stone built up to about 16 feet above flood level. They also developed a new type of windmill. The Dutch version of this machine had four long arms with canvas sails that were turned by the power of the wind. To drain the land, people built dikes around a marshy area and then used the windmills to pump out the water.

When grain is poured into the hopper of a mill, it goes down a chute to the two round millstones that grind it into flour. The force of the running water turns the outside wheel, which powers the machinery inside.

As business and trade increased during the Middle Ages, the need for standards of money and banking became apparent. Merchants traveled great distances to sell their goods, and people needed ways to pay for these items. Sometimes, when people lacked the funds to buy what they needed, they looked for ways to borrow money.

Paper money did not exist in the Middle Ages. Metal coins were the only type of currency used. Coins were made from gold, silver, and copper, and their value was based on the value of these metals. Gold

Banking services were often provided by wealthy individuals or families. This painting is called The Money Changer and His Wife.

coins had the highest value, followed by silver coins. The least valuable were the copper coins. Because this standard was accepted throughout the medieval world, the coins of one region could be exchanged for money or goods from another region. Many distinctive coins were MINTED during the Middle Ages. Coins produced in Islamic regions, for example, had unique patterns with Arabic writing from the Qur'an—the sacred book of Islam.

At first, wealthy individuals acted as bankers, exchanging money and making loans. But as trade expanded across national borders, commercial institutions developed to provide full banking services. These early banks first arose in the cities located along busy trade routes. In the Islamic world, merchants themselves often became involved in the banking business. They provided a money exchange service for which they charged a fee. Muslim commercial law also allowed for a credit transfer, which was similar to a check. It was a way to pay for something without having cash on hand. By the late Middle Ages, the informal methods of moneylending and currency exchange developed into a more formal type of banking. Modern banking first began in the bustling northern Italian towns. (See also *Trade.*)

Mongol Empire

Before the Mongols built their empire, they were a people who herded sheep and horses on the plains of central Asia. That began to change in 1206, when Temüjin, the son of a Mongol chief, was proclaimed Genghis Khan, which means "universal ruler." As the new chief, Genghis Khan began to reorganize and strengthen the military. All Mongol men were required to serve.

In the early 1200s, Genghis Khan and his warriors set out to expand their territory. They invaded and conquered neighboring lands, one by one. Skilled in SIEGE warfare, Mongol warriors used sandbags to fill in moats and ladders to climb fortress walls. If the people of a city resisted, the Mongols ruthlessly killed them. The reputation of the Mongols inspired such fear that many cities simply surrendered rather than face the terrifying consequences. In the 1220s, Mongol armies under Genghis Khan and his generals attacked regions farther west, including Afghanistan, parts of Iraq and Iran, southern Russia, and the Crimea. But then, in 1227, Genghis Khan died suddenly in the midst of planning the final conquest of China.

After his death, Genghis Khan's sons and grandson divided the Mongol Empire. Ogodai, one of Genghis Khan's sons, invaded Eastern Europe and Russia. By the time of Ogodai's death in 1241, the Ukraine and Russia were under Mongol rule. After that, however, arguments broke out among Genghis Khan's remaining heirs. For several years, no one was chosen to be the next great-khan because no single person had enough military support.

In 1279, Kublai Khan completed the Mongol conquest of China that his grandfather had started. Kublai Khan founded the Yuan dynasty, which ruled China for nearly a century. Under Yuan rule, the Mongol Empire had reached its greatest expansion.

Kublai Khan died in 1294, and the empire separated into various territories. In the late 1300s the Mongol conqueror Tamerlane tried to rebuild the empire to its former greatness. Despite his temporary successes, divisions continued, and the Mongol Empire never again achieved unity.

Mongol warriors are shown here storming a Chinese fortress. China fell in the late 1200s. Mongol rule during the next century marked the first time that China was governed by non-Chinese conquerors. The orderly Chinese society was subjected to the attitudes and policies of foreigners, whom they considered to be barbarians. However, the Mongol conquest of China opened that country to trade and contacts with Europe.

Monks, Friars, and Nuns

Monks, friars, and nuns were members of medieval religious orders. Monks and friars were men; nuns were women. Monks lived in monasteries, and friars, at first, lived as wanderers, often sleeping in wooded areas outside of towns. If a man wanted to become a monk, he joined a specific monastery, where he stayed for the rest of his life. A man who wanted to be a friar joined a religious order rather than a particular community.

Although there were similarities between monks and friars,

Monks and nuns, as shown here, chose to lead a religious life in monasteries and convents—communities of like-minded people.

many differences also existed. Monks were not allowed to own any property, but the monastery could—and usually did—own land. Monks led solitary lives of prayer, and they had little contact with the world outside the monastery.

A friar, on the other hand, lived in the world and depended on the charity of others for his living. The word *friar* comes from the Latin word *frater,* which means "brother." Friars could not own property, and neither could the order. At first, friars traveled from town to town, preaching and begging during the day. Eventually, however, the pope allowed them to use Church property and houses that came to be called friaries.

For young women of European medieval society, an alternative to marriage was to enter a convent—a religious home for women. Doing so had significant advantages. In a convent, a woman could receive an education and have a career. She could also engage in prayer with other DE-VOUT women to help save the souls of other people. (See also *Christianity; Women.*)

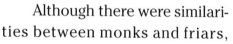

Mysticism

Mystics are people who seek a highly personal relationship with God or some universal truth. Spiritual experiences they describe include seeing visions, hearing inner voices, or feeling a spirit within them. Jewish mystics (Hasidim) achieve their closeness to God through vigorous prayer; Muslim mystics (Sufis) create a trancelike state through poetry, music, and dancing.

Muhammad

The PROPHET Muhammad was the founder of the religion of Islam. He was born in Mecca around 570. Both of his parents died when he was very young, so Muhammad was raised by other family members. When he was about 25 years old, Muhammad married a wealthy widow.

One day, while Muhammad was engaged in deep and serious thought in a cave, he had a vision. An angel told him that he was a messenger of God and gave him a message for the people of Mecca. Throughout his life Muhammad received many such divine messages, or revelations. These revelations became the foundation of Islam and were recorded in the Qur'an—the Islamic book of sacred writings.

Based on his revelations, Muhammad began preaching to the people of Mecca. He taught that there was only one God and that God would judge people on the Last Day. Many people were opposed to Muhammad's message, but his clan protected him. When the chief of his clan died, however, the new chief was unwilling to protect him. Fearing that his life was in danger if he stayed, Muhammad fled to the city of Medina, where he had support from a group of followers. Muhammad made this journey in 622, and it became known as the hegira, which means "flight." The hegira marks the first year of the Islamic calendar.

In the years that followed, the people of Mecca and the Muslims (as Muhammad's followers were called) engaged in a series of battles. Then, in 630, Muhammad led the Muslims into Mecca, and the city gave up without a struggle. Most of the people in Mecca accepted Muhammad as a prophet. Although Muhammad died in 632, Muslims continued to carry his teachings—sometimes by conquest—to many other regions. Today, Islam is one of the world's major religions. (See also *Pilgrimage.*)

Muhammad's teaching became the basis of the Islamic religion. This painting shows Muhammad ascending to heaven.

Music and Dance

There were two kinds of music during the Middle Ages—religious music for worship and other purposes and non-religious, or SECULAR, music for entertainment. Very little medieval secular music was written down. Much more religious music was written down, so more of it has survived.

An important part of medieval church music was the Gregorian chant, also known as plainsong. The name comes from the story that Pope Gregory I received this music from God and gave it to the Church. These chants, which were based on passages from the Bible, required everyone to sing the same notes, without musical accompaniment. Later, organs, choirs, and harmony were added to religious music.

Music was played throughout medieval society. Traveling entertainers called jongleurs sang and played musical instruments. They also juggled, performed acrobatic tricks, and told stories. They often sang about current events and thus kept people informed about happenings in other towns. Other entertainers, known as minstrels, played instruments and sang poetic songs called ballads. Some minstrels worked for noble households, while others—wandering minstrels—traveled from place to place. Troubadours were poet-singers who entertained wealthy families with songs about love and adventure.

Music was also important in the medieval Islamic world. Much of this music was for religious purposes, such as the chant that called Muslims to prayer. Other religious music included songs from the Qur'an (the Islamic holy book), songs for Muslims going on pilgrimages, and songs describing the life of Muhammad (the founder of Islam).

Medieval Muslims also had secular music. They had songs to celebrate special events, such as marriages and births; war songs to inspire the soldiers before going into battle; love songs; and caravan songs.

Surviving music from other traditions tends to be religious. But it is certain that secular music was important in these traditions, too. Jewish medieval music has mostly survived as chants of biblical text, HYMNS, and prayers. Byzantine and Russian music from the Middle Ages is almost exclusively sacred,

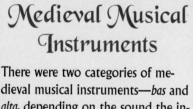

Medieval Musical Instruments

There were two categories of medieval musical instruments—*bas* and *alta*, depending on the sound the instrument created. *Bas* instruments, which usually accompanied singing, made a soft or low sound. The harp, flute, and lute are all *bas* instruments. *Alta* instruments were most often played outdoors. They made loud, high sounds. Trumpets, horns, and bagpipes are *alta* instruments.

Although dancing was condemned by the Catholic Church, it was a popular form of entertainment during the Middle Ages.

or religious, music. But in Scotland, Ireland, and Wales, singing poets called bards entertained people with songs about national history and members of the royal family.

Medieval people frequently danced at social events—such as weddings, tournaments, and other celebrations—and at religious events, such as festivals. Sometimes the dances were accompanied by singers, but at other times only musical instruments were used.

Medieval dances were usually performed by couples or groups of people, rarely by individuals. Some dances were performed in a circle while people sang songs in rounds. Other dances involved jumping and leaping into the air. In the late Middle Ages, the *basse danse* became popular among the noble classes. This stately dance involved a complicated series of steps in which the feet stayed close to the ground.

Medieval musicians, especially trumpeters, performed several practical jobs. They were hired to sound alarms when their city was in danger or to play ceremonial fanfares from the clock tower to announce the time of day.

Nobles and Knights

Europeans who had large landholdings and great wealth were known as nobles during the Middle Ages. They were members of the second highest social class, after kings and queens. Nobles and their families were leaders in their communities and held positions of great power and prestige. Nobility was inherited, which means that it was passed down from parent to child. In the 1100s the nobility became a social class recognized by law.

By that time, many noble families in Europe had begun to face serious problems of survival. Because titles of nobility were inherited,

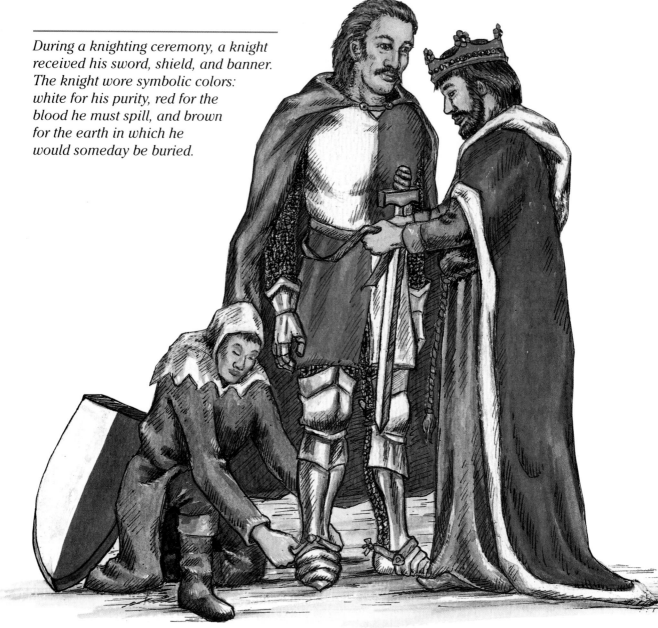

During a knighting ceremony, a knight received his sword, shield, and banner. The knight wore symbolic colors: white for his purity, red for the blood he must spill, and brown for the earth in which he would someday be buried.

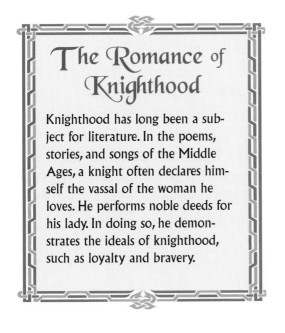
the high infant death rate was an important factor in the decline of the nobility. Since the children of many noble families failed to survive past childhood, few were left to inherit the family lands and titles. As a result, many noble families simply ceased to exist.

In some places, inheritance laws and customs also presented problems for the nobles. With each new generation, more of the wealth and property was divided up, so little remained to support the family. Not all noble families had these problems, however. Some families had such great wealth that it lasted through many generations. Other families arranged to increase their wealth through marriage with another wealthy family.

In the late 900s, knights emerged as a new social class. Knights were armed men who were hired to defend the castles of the nobles. At first, knights formed a class between the nobles and the peasants. Gradually, however, the status of knights improved, and by the end of the Middle Ages, they were often at the same social (if not legal) level as the nobility.

Boys of noble birth began training for knighthood when they were around seven or eight years old. Often they were sent to the home of another noble family, where they could train with other boys. Training for knighthood included learning to ride a horse, use a sword and spear, carry a shield, and wear armor.

Although most sons of nobles trained for knighthood, not all became knights. The cost of becoming a knight was very great. A knight had to supply his own horse, clothing, arms, and armor—all expensive items. Therefore, many young noblemen postponed the knighting ceremony until they could afford to become knights. Others never became knights at all.

Even after becoming a knight, a man needed a way to support himself if his family lacked the means. For this reason, many young men became professional warriors. They offered their loyalty and military skills to whichever lord could afford them. To advertise their combat skills, they entered tournaments. These mock battles provided an opportunity to earn money and demonstrate their fighting skills. (See also *Feudalism; Peasants and Serfs.*)

Normans

Although they started out as Viking raiders from Scandinavia, the Normans eventually became the rulers of northwestern France. Their descendants later ruled England and Sicily (an island off the coast of Italy).

In the 800s, Vikings began raiding towns along the Seine River in France. Eventually, King Charles III the Simple of France met with Rollo, the leader of the Vikings, to arrange a treaty to end the raids. The king gave Rollo and the Vikings a large region north of Paris. In return, the Vikings agreed to convert to Christianity and to defend France against other invaders. The Vikings, who were known as Northmen or Normans, called their new land Normandy.

In the 1000s the Normans made another great conquest. It began with the marriage of Emma, daughter of Duke Richard I of Normandy, to King Ethelred the Unready of England. When their son

This detail from the Bayeux Tapestry shows the Norman cavalry attacking a hill defended by the English. The tapestry is over 230 feet long and shows 72 scenes of medieval life.

Edward the Confessor, who was half Norman, became king of England, the Normans had a claim to the English crown.

In 1066, King Edward died without leaving an heir. The Norman duke, William the Conqueror, claimed the throne, but he was opposed by an English earl. The Norman and English armies fought a fierce battle at Hastings, which the Normans won. The Battle of Hastings was the most famous battle in English history. William was crowned king of England. With only brief interruptions, Normandy and England were united under the same ruler for the next 150 years.

The Battle of Hastings marked a turning point in history. It brought about a new political order in Europe. In addition, England was brought into closer contact with Europe because of the Normans' strong connections with France. During the period of Norman rule in England, great advances were made in art and architecture. One of the most important of these was the spread of an architectural style called Romanesque.

In the late 1000s, Normans began to hire themselves out as fighters in southern Italy against Byzantines and Muslims. They captured Sicily from the Muslims in the 1070s and established a strong kingdom there. To celebrate their conquest of Sicily, they built churches and castles in the Byzantine style.

Omar Khayyam

Omar Khayyam was a poet, mathematician, and ASTRONOMER. He was born in Persia (present-day Iran) in 1048. The name *Khayyam* means "tentmaker" and probably reflects the trade of his father. During his lifetime Omar Khayyam was known for reforming the Islamic calendar. Many years after his death, however, he was better remembered for his poetry. His most famous work is a collection of poems called the *Rubaiyat*. The Arab word *ruba'i* refers to a four-line verse called a quatrain. In a quatrain, the first, second, and fourth lines rhyme.

The poems are about reality, the beauty of nature, and the shortness of life. In 1859, Edward FitzGerald, an English poet, translated the *Rubaiyat* from the original Persian. Some of the verses have become well known, including this one:

> *A book of verses underneath the Bough*
> *A Jug of wine, a Loaf of Bread—and Thou*
> *Beside me singing in the Wilderness—*
> *Oh Wilderness were Paradise enow [enough]!*

Ordeals

During the early Middle Ages, an ordeal was a way of determining the guilt or innocence of a person accused of a crime. Because people believed that God rewarded good deeds and punished wicked ones, the outcome of an ordeal was considered to be a judgment from God.

There were several types of ordeals. In the ordeal by fire, the accused person—after the appropriate blessings—had to hold a hot iron or plunge a hand into a pot of boiling water. The person's hand was burned or scalded, but if the judges decided that it had become infected, the person was found guilty.

In the ordeal by water, the accused individual was bound and thrown into a pool that had been blessed. Those who floated were considered guilty. Those who sank were taken from the water, declared innocent, and freed. Those who were found innocent were often exiled. The belief was that their conduct had been so suspicious that they could never be good members of the community.

An ordeal by combat involved two people who told conflicting stories. They were made to fight until one was the clear winner. His story was considered true. During the 1200s, under pressure from the Church, ordeals gradually came to be replaced by other types of trials. (See also *Heresy and the Inquisition.*)

Papacy

The term *papacy* refers to the office of the pope, who is the highest official in the Roman Catholic Church. When Christianity began, the church was led by several bishops. The title of *pope* was introduced in the 300s, but it was sometimes used for any bishop. It was another 700 years before the term came to be used for only one person—the bishop of Rome.

In the early years of Christianity, Rome was the model for other Christian communities. The city was at the center of the Roman Empire, which gave it cultural and political importance. By the early Middle Ages, the bishops in Rome were held in high esteem. When Gregory I was elected pope in 590, he was influential in both the religious and nonreligious matters of Rome.

The power of the papacy continued to grow throughout the Middle Ages. In the 700s the Frankish king Pepin III gave Italian lands to the pope, making the pope the SECULAR ruler of Italy. After Pope Leo III crowned Charlemagne in 800, the popes in Rome claimed the right to crown emperors and grant them their authority. In exchange, the emperors agreed to defend the popes against attacks from outside the Church.

The power of the papacy began to decline in the 900s as German emperors and Italian factions began to choose their own popes. In the 1000s the popes regained some of their authority when they began changing certain church practices. For example, to prevent outside influence in papal elections, Pope Nicholas II declared a new policy in which only cardinals—high church officials—could elect a new pope. The power of the papacy reached its highest point in the early 1200s.

This painting shows Pope Sylvester I (on horseback) bestowing a blessing on the emperor Constantine I. According to legend, Constantine converted to Christianity after Sylvester cured him of a terrible disease.

Parliament

During the Middle Ages, the English king had a council of advisers made up of nobles and high church officials. Sometimes the council was increased in number by the addition of knights representing the people in the countryside and townsmen representing the people in urban areas.

Beginning in the 1250s, large meetings of the great council, or parliaments, became more frequent because the king used them to publicize his policies and especially to convince the representatives of the countryside and towns to agree to taxes. Other matters were considered by only the king and the lords and high churchmen, who together made up the king's high court, and they accepted or rejected requests from the town and rural representatives for changes in the law. Because the groups had such different duties, they met separately. Eventually, in the 1400s, the nobles and high churchmen became the House of Lords, and the representatives from the towns and countryside became the House of Commons.

King Edward I of England is shown here presiding over his Parliament. Edward enlarged Parliament to include representatives of towns and rural areas.

At the end of the Middle Ages, the House of Lords was far more important than the House of Commons. However, there could be no general taxation without the consent of the Commons. (See also *Peasants and Serfs.*)

Patrick

So many legends exist about the life of Saint Patrick, as he is now called, that he has become a mysterious figure in Irish history. Born in Britain around A.D. 389, Patrick was the son of a church DEACON and the grandson of a priest. When he was about 16, Patrick was captured in a raid and forced into slavery in Ireland. After spending six years as a slave, he escaped and returned to his family. He decided to become a MISSIONARY and return to Ireland. In 431 the pope sent Palladius, a bishop, on a mission to Ireland. When Palladius died soon afterward, Patrick was named as his replacement.

Patrick's most famous work is called the *Confession*. In it he defended himself against a charge that had been leveled against him. He also discussed his belief that he had been chosen by God for his mission in Ireland. During the 30 years that Patrick spent traveling and preaching throughout the country, he helped convert many people to Christianity. Saint Patrick's Day is celebrated every year on March 17 in his honor.

Peasants and Serfs

Medieval society was divided between people who lived in towns and people who lived in the countryside. Some of those who lived in the countryside were very wealthy. They had huge estates and were recognized by the law as nobles—superior to other people. Most people in the country, however, were farmers and laborers. These people are often called peasants by those who study the Middle Ages. Peasants made up about 90 percent of all people in medieval Europe.

Many peasants were serfs who were owned by wealthy lords. They had to do certain work for their owners, such as planting and harvesting the lord's crops. There were also certain things a serf could not do. For example, a serf could not become a priest or a nun without the permission of his or her lord. The son or daughter of a serf was automatically a serf. But a serf was not a slave—a person with no rights at all. No lord could rightfully kill a serf, except in self-defense, without the decision of a court that the serf was guilty of a crime legally punishable by death.

In the 1200s, many lords in Western Europe allowed serfs to buy their freedom for money. Even so, serfdom continued beyond the Middle Ages in Western Europe. In Eastern Europe in the late Middle Ages, serfdom became even more widespread and harsher. In one form or another, serfdom lasted in some regions until the 1860s. (See also *Feudalism; Slavery.*)

Sometimes the harsh conditions of peasant life led to open rebellion, as shown here, against the king or local lord.

Pilgrimage

A person who travels to a holy place for a religious purpose is called a pilgrim. The journey is called a pilgrimage. Christians, Muslims, and Jews all went on pilgrimages during the Middle Ages, although the purposes and destinations of these trips were different.

Christians had three main reasons for making pilgrimages: to prepare their souls for life after death; to repent, or show that they were sorry for

People belonging to every social class—from kings to peasants—made pilgrimages. This illustration from Chaucer's Canterbury Tales shows a group of pilgrims on their way to the shrine of St. Thomas Becket.

their sins; and to visit the SHRINES of saints and other holy figures. Shrines held sacred objects that were associated with saints. People believed that these objects could work miracles, such as curing disease. For Christian pilgrims the most popular destination was Jerusalem, where Jesus Christ had died. The second most popular destination was Rome, where the bodies of Saint Peter and Saint Paul are buried.

Since the founding of Islam in the 600s, it has been the religious duty of all Muslims to make a hajj—a pilgrimage to Mecca—at least once in their lifetimes. For Muslims, Mecca is the holiest city because it was the birthplace of Muhammad, the founder of Islam. At a certain time of the year, Islamic pilgrims from around the world make the hajj to Mecca. In the Middle Ages they traveled overland in large CARAVANS from Egypt, Syria, and Muslim regions of North Africa.

Jerusalem was the most common destination for Jewish pilgrims. Jerusalem is important to Jews because it is the site of King Solomon's Temple. Because of certain ancient Jewish customs, pilgrimages often occurred in autumn. Jews prayed at the Temple Mount in Jerusalem, where King Solomon's Temple once stood and where the Second Temple later stood, until the Romans destroyed it in the year 70. (See also *Saints and Relics.*)

Reconquest of Spain

In the year 711, followers of Islam invaded Spain from North Africa. These Muslim invaders, known as Moors, conquered most of Spain within a few years. Some Spanish Christians in the north remained independent of the Moors, and over the next 700 years, they fought to reconquer Spain.

During the long peace following the Moors' conquest, science, medicine, and mathematics flourished in Spain. Muslims had preserved the writings of ancient philosophers, such as Aristotle. In Spain, they built schools that provided free education for the poor. Moorish cities were famous for producing fine metalwork, leather, silk, and glass. In the 1000s, however, the Moors began to fight among themselves. They split into many small kingdoms, weakening their hold on Spain.

Spaniards from the north attacked the weakened and divided Moors. The Kingdom of Castile, named for the many castles located on its frontier, led the fight to push the Muslim invaders out of Spain. The legendary Spanish hero known as El Cid, who fought many victorious battles against the Moors, came from Castile. By the mid-1200s the Spaniards had captured the Moorish capital of Córdoba, and only the southern port city of Grenada remained under Muslim control.

In the late 1400s the marriage of Queen Isabella of Castile and King Ferdinand of Aragon united most of Spain. Their troops conquered Grenada the same year they sent explorer Christopher Columbus on the voyage that took him to the Americas—1492.

Although the Moors were no longer in power, their culture remained important. The writings of Greek, Roman, and Middle Eastern philosophers that the Moors had preserved and translated spread throughout Europe. Muslim houses of worship, called MOSQUES, and intricately designed palaces, called alcazars, still stand in the cities the Moors once ruled. Today, however, they are used for different purposes. (See also *Alhambra; Islam; Warfare.*)

It took more than 700 years for Spanish Christians to regain Spain from Muslim invaders. Shown here are battleships filled with Spanish warriors.

Rome

This overview of medieval Rome shows the Colosseum (circular building) and other important buildings and monuments.

Rome—the capital of the ancient and powerful Roman Empire—was ravaged by a series of Germanic invasions in the 400s. The city lost its former prestige and Rome fell into a serious state of disrepair. Many of its public buildings were closed and its government barely functioned. Even so, Rome remained an important pilgrimage site as the place where the apostles Peter and Paul were buried.

In 590, Gregory—a monk and scholar—became pope. He tried to stop the city's decline, with some success. In the 700s, however, the Lombards (a Germanic tribe) seized some of the surrounding towns, and an attack on Rome seemed likely. But the Frankish king, Charlemagne, vowed to protect the city. On Christmas Day in 800, Charlemagne was crowned Roman emperor by Pope Leo III. With the support of the Franks, the city thrived.

The early 800s were prosperous years for Rome. But then a Muslim attack on the city set off another period of decline. After this attack, Pope Leo IX built a wall around the papal offices. In 962, the German king, Otto I the Great, offered to protect the pope from the unhappy citizens of Rome. The pope was so grateful that he crowned Otto emperor of the region that would later become known as the Holy Roman Empire.

By the 1000s the papacy had grown stronger and had taken control of Rome. But a dispute arose between the pope and the German ruler over the appointment of bishops. After some fighting and the destruction by fire of sections of the city, the Germans regained control of Rome. They urged the citizens of Rome to elect their own leaders, which led to problems between the papacy and the city government.

In the early 1300s the papacy was moved to Avignon, France. By the end of the century, however, not only had the papacy been returned to Rome but Pope Boniface IX had claimed papal control over that city's government.

A saint is a person who is officially declared holy by the Christian Church. In the early years of Christianity, a saint was usually a martyr—someone who had suffered greatly and died rather than give up his or her religious faith. People believed that miracles had occurred at the time of the martyr's death, and they honored the martyr by leaving gifts at his or her burial site. In this way ordinary Christians informally declared a person's sainthood. The early church leaders did not officially recognize these saints.

In the Middle Ages, the Church acquired control over who could be considered a saint. Special tombs were made for the saints' bodies, and each saint had an official day on the church calendar. When a person was nominated for sainthood, or canonization, a committee investigated the individual's life and made a recommendation to the pope. The pope then decided whether to grant sainthood.

This painting shows Saint Veronica holding the veil with which she is said to have wiped the face of Jesus.

Saints in Art

In Christian art, saints are often shown with a halo—a circle of glowing light around the saint's head. Jesus Christ is also shown this way. Some saints are shown with a symbol by which they are identified. For example, Jesus was said to have given Saint Peter the keys to the kingdom of heaven. Peter is often shown with two keys. The study and identification of these symbols is called iconography.

During the Middle Ages, veneration—a show of deep respect—of saints was common. People wrote about saints, depicted them in paintings and sculpture, and dedicated SHRINES to them. These memorials, or remembrances, encouraged Christians to lead lives worthy of the saints.

Veneration of relics was another way for the faithful to show their devotion. Relics are the remains of the bodies of saints and of objects associated with saints, such as clothing and crosses. Because many people believed—and still do—that relics can perform miracles, they prayed for miracles at shrines. Many shrines became destinations for pilgrimages.

Saladin

Saladin, the greatest Muslim hero of the Middle Ages, was born around 1137. As a young man he joined his father and brother in the service of Nur al-Din, a Syrian SULTAN. Saladin took part in three military campaigns against Egypt. His success in battle led to his promotion to commander of the Syrian army in Egypt and appointment as VIZIER—head of the Muslim government in Egypt.

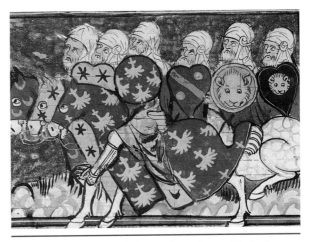

Saladin recaptured Jerusalem from Christian Crusaders. This painting shows soldiers in Saladin's army.

Saladin reformed the Egyptian economy and military forces. After Nur al-Din died in 1174, Saladin extended his rule into Syria, Iraq, and neighboring regions. He then turned his attention to the Christian Crusaders who had captured Jerusalem. In 1187, Saladin and his army defeated the Crusaders at the Battle of Hittin and then went on to recapture Jerusalem.

In an attempt to retake Jerusalem, Western European Christians launched the Third Crusade. The Crusaders never recaptured the holy city, but their attacks hurt Saladin's forces. In 1192, Saladin and Richard I the Lionhearted made a peace treaty. Saladin died soon afterward—greatly admired by Muslims and respected by many Christians as well.

Scholasticism

Scholasticism was a way of thinking and teaching that began in Western Europe in the 1000s. Scholasticism sought to combine ancient philosophy and worldly knowledge with Christian beliefs. Some parts of the Bible seemed to disagree with other parts. In addition, the ideas of some respected authorities, such as the ancient Greek philosopher Aristotle, sometimes conflicted with the Bible. The goal of scholasticism was to analyze these texts in detail and then use reason and logic to interpret them.

Scholasticism reached its peak in the 1200s in the universities of Europe. Students were taught to consider all sides of a question and then to state their own arguments. Critics complained that the scholastic method was too formal and that it gave the mistaken impression that all problems could be solved by reason. (See also *Aquinas, Thomas.*)

Schools and Universities

During the Middle Ages, only select groups of people attended school, and most of them learned only basic skills. Some schools offered training for certain professions. Institutions of higher education—colleges and universities—did not appear until the late 1100s.

Most schools in medieval Europe were supported by the Church. Cathedral schools trained young men to become church officials or priests. Monastic schools provided Christian instruction for the monks who lived in monasteries. Students first learned basic reading, writing, and arithmetic skills. Then they studied Latin and the Bible. Many monks became teachers themselves, and some even taught kings and their children.

The first European colleges were established in Italy and France, and others soon followed in England, Spain, and Germany. At first, colleges were residences for students. Universities were often far from students' homes, and colleges provided a place to eat and sleep. As the number of students living in these residences increased, colleges became centers of learning and parts of a university. Students began their university studies when they were about 14 years old. They were taught grammar, math, and PHILOSOPHY. Medieval universities used two teaching methods—lectures and disputations. In lecture halls, students listened to their schoolmaster speak on a particular subject. In disputations, which were similar to debates, students argued for or against a statement presented by the master.

Muslim colleges began in the 600s—many centuries before they appeared in Western Europe. Students learned about Islamic law, Arabic grammar, and the Qur'an—the holy book of Islam. At first, colleges were located in mosques—Muslim houses of worship—and attended by local students. Later, however, inns were built so that students from other regions had a place to live while they attended school.

Education was also important to medieval Jews. In northern Europe, the main focus of Jewish education was religious study, specifically study of the Talmud—the book of Jewish learning and religious law. Jewish schools in the Islamic world and in Spain often combined Jewish studies with academic subjects, such as mathematics, science, and philosophy.

In the early Middle Ages, Babylonia was the largest Jewish community. It was home to great Jewish academies called yeshivas, where scholars studied the Talmud. The leaders of these academies were highly respected. In the 1000s, as the yeshivas in Babylonia declined, new academies developed in other countries, including Germany, France, and Spain.

Unlike the colleges and universities in Europe, higher education in the Byzantine Empire did not usually occur in formal settings. Instead, most students had private teachers. However, Byzantine institutions of higher education did exist. For example, there were schools for professional training in law.

Most European education in the Middle Ages promoted greater understanding of the Bible. Reading, writing, Latin, and music were also important subjects.

Science and Technology

Several factors contributed to the growth and spread of scientific knowledge during the Middle Ages. Islamic scholars translated ancient Greek scientific texts into Arabic. Jewish scholars translated these works into Hebrew, and later scholars translated them into Latin. These translations helped to spread the science of ancient Greece—as well as Jewish and Islamic science—to Western Europe. By studying these works, medieval scholars developed many new scientific traditions and made significant advances in TECHNOLOGY.

Islamic science began in earnest in the mid-700s, when Muslim scholars began to translate ancient Greek texts into Arabic. In order to expand their knowledge of ASTRONOMY, Islamic scholars built complex instruments, such as sundials and astrolabes, with which to observe the movements of the planets and other heavenly bodies.

Islamic scientists played a major role in the history of technology. They developed hard soap as well as new and easier ways to manufacture cloth and paper. Islamic engineers designed and constructed irrigation systems, fountains, clocks, and other mechanical devices.

Many Jewish scholars worked alongside Islamic scientists, translating medical and scientific texts from Arabic into Hebrew. They also made significant progress in the fields of mathematics and astronomy. Abraham bar Hiyya wrote the first European algebra text in the early 1100s. Jewish astronomer Levi ben Gershom accurately calculated the distances between the planets in the 1300s.

The Byzantines developed two remarkable inventions: automata and Greek fire. Automata were mechanical devices, similar to robots, that mimicked lions roaring and birds singing. They were displayed in the imperial palace in Constantinople for the amusement of visitors. Greek fire was an oily substance that was sprayed on enemy ships to set them on fire. The Byzantines also invented the glass counterweight, which was used by merchants for weighing their merchandise.

Around the year 800, advances in technology gained interest among Europeans, who began using scientific principles to solve specific problems. Over the next centuries, medieval Europeans improved water mills and plows. They developed the

Alchemy

Alchemy, a chemical science of the Middle Ages, aimed to produce gold and silver from less precious metals. Alchemists used techniques similar to those used by modern scientists to perform their experiments. But alchemists believed that their success depended in part on spiritual purity and on finding the magical elixir that could change lesser metals into gold—and maybe even prolong life.

This illustration is from a medieval book of hymns. It shows an astronomer (in the center), a mathematician, and a scribe, who is taking notes.

flying buttress to support cathedral walls and developed a new type of windmill, an improved horse collar, and the PRINTING PRESS. They also contributed to the development of several scientific instruments, including the compass and the hourglass. Advances in technology in one field often gave rise to advancements in another. For example, the technology used in the ancient Roman crossbow was improved by medieval Europeans and eventually used to make the coiled springs in clocks. (See also *Gutenberg, Johannes; Maps and Mapmaking; Medicine.*)

91

Seals and signets are identifying marks or designs stamped onto hot wax or metal. In the Middle Ages they were widely used to AUTHENTICATE official documents or close important packages. Although wax was used for the majority of seals, gold, lead, and silver were also used. Documents were written on parchment—a paperlike material made from the skin of sheep or goats—and wax seals were usually attached to them by a hanging cord. Sometimes hot wax was applied directly to the document, and a ring (signet) or another piece of engraved metal was pressed on it, leaving an image.

The use of seals and signets dates back to well before the Middle Ages and was common in ancient Rome. In the early Middle Ages only kings used wax seals to verify that official documents were genuine. In the 800s, high church leaders such as bishops were permitted to use seals to prove the authenticity of their documents. A century later, personal seals and signets were used by princes and nobles.

At first, seals served no legal purpose. As time passed, however, the seal became legal proof that a document was genuine. The use of seals became common among a wide range of groups and individuals, including universities, the Church, merchants, and town officials. Toward the end of the Middle Ages, seals were used less and less. Eventually a handwritten signature became a common way to show that a document was authentic.

Seals and signets were used to authenticate important documents. The seal shown here was used by the Scottish king Robert I the Bruce in the early 1300s.

Slavery

Slavery—the ownership of one human being by another—existed during ancient times and continued into, and well beyond, the Middle Ages. Medieval Christians believed that master and slave should not be of the same ethnic group. During the early Middle Ages, Christians came into conflict with non-Christians in central and northern Europe and some English, German, and Scandinavian people were

This painting shows a slave market in the Islamic city of Baghdad. Some Islamic slaves rose to positions of high rank in the military.

captured and enslaved. Many European Christian and non-Christian slaves were sold to Muslims. Eventually many non-Christian Europeans converted to Christianity, and slavery began to decline. At the same time, the number of serfs (rural workers owned by wealthy lords) increased.

In the Islamic world, slavery was considered acceptable and natural. According to both the Qur'an (the Islamic book of sacred writings) and Muslim law, God created inequalities between people—between master and slave, and between man and woman. But the Qur'an also advises masters to treat slaves well and to set them free as an act of kindness.

Slaves in Islamic society most often worked for families who lived in cities. They performed a variety of household tasks, such as cooking, cleaning, and caring for children. Some were even responsible for a household's financial matters. Slaves in the Islamic world were generally better off than slaves in other societies, where they were used for farm labor.

The Islamic idea of slavery was to bring outsiders into the Muslim community through conversion to Islam. Slavery was meant to be temporary, ending with the granting of freedom, or manumission, usually when a young slave became an adult. (See also *Aztec Empire; Peasants and Serfs.*)

Tamerlane

Tamerlane, also known as Timur Lenk or Timur the Lame, was a Mongol conqueror in the 1300s. A great—but cruel—leader, he tried to rebuild the Mongol Empire of the 1200s by invading and conquering much of central Asia and the Middle East.

Tamerlane became a chief in 1361. Using military strategies developed by Genghis Khan, he soon conquered Iran, Armenia, and Mesopotamia. In 1398, Tamerlane invaded India and massacred many people. He then moved on to Syria, where he took Damascus.

Tamerlane died in 1405 while planning a conquest of China. Because he had not established governments in the regions he conquered, they were left unprotected and were conquered by others. As a result, Tamerlane's empire fell apart after he died. More than a century after his death, one of his descendants, Babur, founded India's Mughal DYNASTY.

Templars

In 1119 a group of French knights founded the Poor Knights of Christ, an order of knights. After King Baldwin II of Jerusalem gave them lodgings near Solomon's Temple, the order became known as the Knights Templars. One of the group's main responsibilities was to protect pilgrims in the Holy Land. The Templars also became a powerful military force in the Crusades. Bernard of Clairvaux, the leader of the Cistercian order of monks, wrote the rules of the order. The Templars wore the white cloak of the Cistercians with the addition of a red cross.

At the height of their popularity, the Templars had 20,000 members organized into three groups—knights, priests, and townspeople. The order prospered from its banking businesses. But the Templars' great wealth caused envy and resentment, in part leading to their persecution by King Philip IV of France. Many Templars were sent to prison. Some were tortured or burned. In 1312, Pope Clement V dissolved the order. (See also *Teutonic Knights.*)

The Templars formed to protect the Holy Sepulcher, the place where Christ was believed to have been buried.

94

Teutonic Knights

Established in 1190, the Teutonic Knights were the last of the great medieval orders of knights to be formed during the Crusades. Members of the order were German noblemen. They started as a charitable organization, caring for fallen Crusaders in Jerusalem. In 1198, however, the Teutonic Knights became a military order and began fighting the Turks in the Holy Land. The following year, the order was officially recognized by Pope Innocent III. Members wore white cloaks with black crosses. The shields and banners they carried were also adorned with black crosses. Although the Teutonic Knights were few in number, they were greatly respected for their courage and enthusiasm.

Because there were other orders in the Holy Land, the Teutonic Knights began to operate in Eastern Europe. There they took part in a Crusade against the Slavs, a large group of non-Christians who lived in the region. The Teutonic Knights gradually conquered Prussia and forced most of the people to convert to Christianity. Their Headquarters were in Marienburg, the largest castle in Europe. The order remained a powerful force through the 1300s.

Tithes

The word *tithe* comes from an Old English word that means "one-tenth." During the Middle Ages, farmers had to give one-tenth (or ten percent) of their harvest to the Church. Similarly, craftspeople had to give ten percent of their earnings to the Church.

Tithes date back to ancient Israel, where they were used mainly to support religious leaders and sometimes to help the poor. Tithes were not required by the early Christian Church, but by the 500s, church law required them. Throughout the Middle Ages, the tithe was used to support priests and other church officials. Tithes also provided funds for the repair and maintenance of church buildings and for social services, such as education, aid to the poor, and medical care. Most people were willing to pay the tithes because they believed that it was a way to thank God for favors.

Less Than a Tenth

Although few people refused to pay tithes, some were known to underpay them. This was especially true for new converts to Christianity, who were unaware that their conversion came with a financial obligation.

Tournaments and Games

The tournament was the most popular and festive sporting event of the Middle Ages. Tournaments were contests in which knights could show their skill and bravery.

The joust was the favorite event in medieval tournaments. During a joust, two knights in armor would charge at each other on horseback. Each knight carried a lance with a blunt end. It differed from the lance used in battle, which had a sharp steel point at the end. The object of the joust was to knock your opponent off his horse by hitting him with the lance.

There were other tournament events as well. During foot combat, knights showed their fencing skills by fighting each other with swords. The *baston* involved pairs or groups of knights on horses. Using blunted swords, they tried to knock the crest off their opponents' helmets. In the melee, groups of knights fought on horseback.

Jousting, also called tilting, was the most popular medieval tournament. In a joust, two armored knights on horseback charged each other with lances. The aim was to knock one's opponent off his horse.

Tournaments are probably the most famous sporting events of the Middle Ages. However, regular citizens also took part in games and sporting events. Since citizens were sometimes called to battle, they had to know how to use weapons. They competed in fencing and archery.

People played peaceful games, too. Many of these were action games similar to those played by children today. Games such as hide-and-seek, blindman's buff, and tug-of-war are modern versions of medieval games. People also played games with balls, but these games were somewhat different from modern ball games. Balls used in medieval times did not bounce. Instead of rubber, these balls were made of fabric or leather with rags stuffed inside.

During the Middle Ages, people also played table games, including card games, dice games, and board games. Some medieval board games, such as chess and backgammon, are still popular.

Muslim Games

Although early Muslims considered games a distraction from the serious business of daily life, they played some games. Children played a game like checkers. Board games such as chess were popular with adults. Skill at chess was a sign of an educated person. Since these games involved strategy and planning, they were considered good training for military leaders. Physical exercise was also considered good training for future warriors.

Trade

Trade is the exchange of goods for other goods or for money. During the Middle Ages, goods produced in one region were carried overland or by water to be traded somewhere else. Some of these goods were things that everyone needed, such as grain and salt. Others were luxury items, such as silk and precious stones. Several cities and regions became important medieval trade centers. Others grew because they were located along major trade routes. Still others became important because they produced goods that were in great demand.

During the early years of the Byzantine Empire, luxury items such as spices and pearls were brought from the Far East. These items were traded in Constantinople and then carried farther west for sale throughout Europe. In the 600s, war and disease caused a decline in the Byzantine population and thus in trade. For example, instead of growing crops for trade, many farmers produced only enough for their own families. By the 1000s, however, new cities began to develop. Older cities such as Constantinople expanded into giant trading centers.

During the Middle Ages, much long-distance trade took place by sea. This illustration shows a busy seaport where goods are loaded for shipping and unloaded for sale.

The spread of Islam created a huge trading empire in the Middle East. The Islamic world extended from Spain and Morocco, across North Africa, and east to India and Asia. Although these regions were very different from one another and were not governed by a single ruler, Islam brought them together as an economic unit. Baghdad was its most important city and trading center. Many exotic goods were traded there. These included silk and paper from China, rubies and panther skins from India, and fine cloth from Egypt.

During the Middle Ages, Western European trade was concentrated in two areas. In northern Europe, the Baltic Sea was a main trade route. In the South, Italy was a major trading center. Although trade included such basic necessities as food, luxury goods such as silk and spices were also traded. (See also *Fairs and Markets.*)

Silk Secrets

Throughout history, silk has been considered an especially valuable fabric. To produce silk, people used a special process involving the eggs of silk moths, which were originally found only in China. The silk-making process was a closely guarded secret in China for more than 2,000 years. Eventually, however, some silk-moth eggs were smuggled out of China, and the secrets of silk making became known throughout the world. By the 1200s, silk was being produced in Italy.

Transportation

During the Middle Ages, people traveled for many reasons, and they used several methods of transportation. The most common reasons for travel included trade and journeys to holy places. People traveled on foot, on horseback, in horse-drawn carts, and by boat.

Before the Middle Ages began, the ancient Romans had built a large network of roads in Europe and the Middle East. This extensive system of roads enabled people to travel safely over great distances in Western Europe and around the Mediterranean. This encouraged trade and the spread of Christianity. After the fall of the Roman Empire in 476, however, long-distance travel decreased considerably.

However, some people—mostly members of the royal and noble classes—continued to travel. Others, such as Christian missionaries,

This mural, painted around a doorway in Italy, shows several types of transportation—horseback, cart, and wagon. Because travelers risked being robbed or killed by bandits, they often traveled in large groups, as shown here. Led by a churchman on horseback, the group in the wagon may be making a pilgrimage to a holy place.

traveled to spread Christianity to non-Christian regions. The towns and churches located along a stretch of road were responsible for its maintenance. Most roads were only dirt paths, and their maintenance usually required minor work, such as the removal of fallen trees. Tolls were imposed on pilgrims, merchants, and other travelers passing over these stretches of road.

In the 700s and early 800s, cargo boats carrying grains, silks, and spices sailed the water routes of Europe. The rivers of France and Germany became important trade routes. Then raids and invasions during the late 800s and 900s resulted in declining trade and travel.

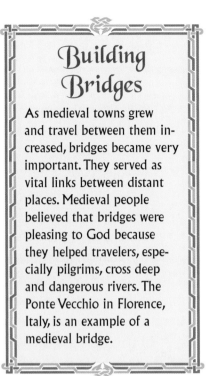

Building Bridges

As medieval towns grew and travel between them increased, bridges became very important. They served as vital links between distant places. Medieval people believed that bridges were pleasing to God because they helped travelers, especially pilgrims, cross deep and dangerous rivers. The Ponte Vecchio in Florence, Italy, is an example of a medieval bridge.

An upswing in the European economy in the 1100s brought another increase in travel. Merchants traveled to distant fairs and markets to buy and sell goods. Some merchants hired people to buy and sell for them. Then they hired other people to move the goods from place to place using packhorses or riverboats. As the number of roads in medieval Europe increased, people began to classify them according to size. In the 1200s, a French writer listed five kinds of roads in use at that time. Included in his list were four-foot-wide roads, called paths, and eight-foot-wide roads, called *carrières*.

Long-distance travel was common in the medieval Islamic world. Muslims made pilgrimages to holy sites; they also traveled for military reasons and for trade. Since ships were sometimes attacked by pirates, and shipwrecks were common, most Muslims preferred to travel by way of the overland routes.

Muslims used pack animals—camels, mules, or donkeys—to transport their belongings. Most wheeled vehicles had disappeared before the rise of Islam. The main reason was that pack animals, particularly camels, were less expensive and more reliable to use. Wheeled carts were expensive to build, and the wood needed to build them was difficult to find in desert regions. Camels, on the other hand, could travel long distances with very little food or water and on nearly any kind of terrain. For safety reasons, people often traveled together in large CARA-VANS. (See also *Cities and Towns; Fairs and Markets.*)

Turks

During the Middle Ages the Turks were a group of NOMADIC peoples who controlled a large area of central Asia. Several Turkish DYNASTIES came to power in different regions of Asia during the medieval period. The Seljuk Turks and the Ottoman Turks were two of the most important dynasties.

In the late 900s, the Seljuk Turks migrated into the region that is present-day Iran. There they learned about the Islamic religion, and many became Muslims. They then conquered most of Iran, Iraq, Armenia, Georgia, and Asia Minor. In 1071 the Seljuk Turks defeated the Byzantine army at the Battle of Manzikert. With this victory the Seljuks gained control over most of Anatolia—the western region of present-day Turkey. As the Seljuks expanded their occupation of the Byzantine Empire, Islam began to replace Christianity in the region.

In the late 1200s and early 1300s, Osman I, chief of the Seljuk Turks, gained control of Anatolia. He founded the dynasty that became known as the Ottomans. In the 1400s, the Ottomans expanded their empire to include territory around the northeast Mediterranean Sea and Black Sea.

In 1453, Ottoman Turks put an end to the Byzantine Empire when they captured Constantinople, the Byzantine capital. The Ottomans ruled over a region that grew into a vast empire. At the peak of its greatness, the Ottoman Empire included Anatolia, Hungary, Crimea, the Balkans, and parts of Arabia, Syria, and North Africa. The Ottoman Empire survived until 1922.

This picture shows Ottoman Turks invading Europe, where they conquered parts of Serbia and Bulgaria. A military defeat in the late 1600s halted Ottoman expansion.

Vikings

The Vikings were a great seafaring people. These Scandinavians—people from Sweden, Denmark, and Norway—raided, explored, and settled many lands during the Middle Ages. They were fierce warriors, and their raids extended from the North Atlantic to Russia.

Around 793, Vikings began raiding the islands in the Irish Sea. They then moved along the coast of Ireland, where they founded permanent settlements. The present-day Irish cities of Dublin, Cork, and Limerick grew from these early medieval settlements.

Their well-constructed ships enabled the Vikings to travel on waterways that many other vessels could not navigate. In the 860s, Vikings sailed to Iceland. Aside from a few Irish monks, the island was uninhabited, and the Vikings had no need to raid or conquer. They settled in Iceland, increased in number, and eventually converted to Christianity.

From Iceland, the Vikings ventured farther into the North Atlantic. Around 1000, under the leadership of Eric the Red, a group settled in Greenland. Years later, Leif Ericson, son of Eric the Red, led an expedition to North America, which he called Vinland. Although some Vikings remained at this site, their settlements did not last long.

While the Vikings from Norway (called Norsemen) were settling lands in Britain, Iceland, and even North America, Danish Vikings were raiding lands in Europe. These raids along the coasts of France, Spain, Italy, and England caused great fear among the inhabitants. Some communities paid money—later called Danegeld in England—to avoid attack. Eventually, King Charles III the Simple of France agreed to let the Danish Vikings settle in Normandy. In return, these Vikings (called Normans) agreed to defend their new land.

Vikings from Sweden sailed east across the Baltic Sea and then south on the rivers of Russia. The land was vast, and few people lived there. These Swedish Vikings were interested in establishing trading links, but they also seem to have established strong principalities in Russia. Through intermarriage they eventually merged with the native Russian population.

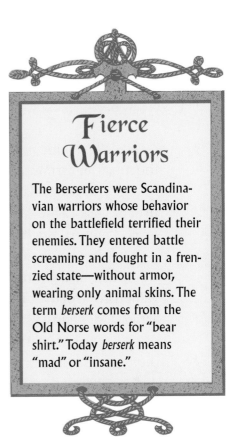

Fierce Warriors

The Berserkers were Scandinavian warriors whose behavior on the battlefield terrified their enemies. They entered battle screaming and fought in a frenzied state—without armor, wearing only animal skins. The term *berserk* comes from the Old Norse words for "bear shirt." Today *berserk* means "mad" or "insane."

Warfare

In the early Middle Ages, fighting occurred both on foot and on horseback. Warriors often fought out of a sense of duty. By the late Middle Ages, weapons became much more powerful and destructive, and many warriors fought because they were paid to do so.

In Western Europe in the early Middle Ages, many kingdoms required that all freemen (people who were not slaves) be available for military service. Noblemen generally were part of the cavalry (horsemen), while peasants were infantry (foot soldiers). In some regions, however, dense forests made it impractical to fight on horseback, so everyone fought as infantry.

In the 700s, the system known as military feudalism developed. Under this system, VASSALS provided military services to their lord in return for his protection and the use of his land. But the weapons and armor needed for military service were expensive. In addition, the vassals needed training to become knights. To ease the burden, the lord provided his vassals with laborers to farm the land he had given to them. Then the vassals could devote their time and resources to the training and equipment they needed to become knights.

After 1200, however, kings began to hire soldiers rather than rely on their lords and vassals to provide military service. These soldiers, called mercenaries, fought for payment rather than out of loyalty to the king. Improvements in weaponry and the development of gunpowder, cannons, and other firearms forever changed the history of warfare.

For most of the Middle Ages, Byzantine warfare was defensive rather than offensive.

A siege tower, like the one at the right, enabled some soldiers to scale the wall, while others shot arrows down on those defending the castle.

Instead of conquering new lands, the Byzantines were more interested in protecting their empire from invaders. Byzantine armies were fairly small, and the leaders relied more on clever military tactics than on numbers of soldiers. Byzantines often worked to end long wars through negotiation rather than victories on the battlefield.

Mongol society was centered on warfare and conquest. As nomads, the Mongols made an excellent invading army. They traveled up to 60 miles a day across the grassy plains of central Asia, which provided food for their horses. The Mongols' skill on horseback and with the bow and arrow enabled them to attack quickly and unleash a storm of arrows on their enemies. Sometimes, Mongol warriors pretended to retreat and then encircled and attacked the pursuing enemy.

Mongol warriors were also skilled in SIEGE warfare. Huge shields protected them from attack as they used storming ladders to climb castle walls and sandbags to fill in moats. If a city resisted invasion, the Mongols killed all the men and forced the women and children to become slaves. The Mongol armies became so widely feared that many cities chose to surrender rather than fight back. (See also *Armor and Weapons; Castles and Fortifications.*)

105

West African Kingdoms

West Africa had many important kingdoms during the Middle Ages. Among the most powerful were Ghana, Mali, Songhai, and Benin.

Ghana was one of the earliest West African kingdoms to emerge during the Middle Ages. Located on the caravan routes that crossed the Sahara, the kingdom reached the height of its power during the early 900s. The king of Ghana was believed to be one of the richest men in the world. He gained power by controlling the trade of salt, copper, gold, ivory, and slaves. By the mid-1000s, Ghana had been conquered by a rival tribe.

Mali was founded in 1240 when King Sundiata destroyed Kumbi, the former capital of Ghana. Mali's power came from its gold mines, which provided much of the world's gold supply. Mali was an Islamic empire. Timbuktu and other large cities in the kingdom became centers of Islamic culture and learning. In 1324, Mali's most powerful king, Mansa Musa, made a famous pilgrimage to Mecca with a CARAVAN of camels loaded with gold. By the 1500s, the kingdom had declined and much of it came under the control of the Songhai kingdom.

During his pilgrimage to Mecca, Mansa Musa of Mali impressed the Arab world with his vast wealth. While in Egypt, he gave away so much gold that he reduced the value of the country's money.

After conquering Mali, Songhai gained control of the trade routes across the Sahara. Songhai kings, including Sunni Ali and Askia Muhammad, created a strong central government that regulated trade and encouraged the people to convert to Islam. The Songhai kingdom fell in 1591 after it was conquered by the Moroccan army.

From the 1200s to the 1800s, the kingdom of Benin ruled the rain forest regions of present-day Nigeria. Wealthy kings, known as *obas*, gained power by controlling trade routes to the south and selling slaves in exchange for European guns. Benin ARTISANS created brass, bronze, and ivory sculptures that are famous for their distinctive style.

106

Women

Most medieval women spent their time at home, running the household and raising children. Women were expected to produce male heirs and to teach household skills to their daughters. However, depending on a woman's social class and religion, she might have an opportunity to pursue her interests or develop her talents in other ways.

In upper-class European society, young women were taught reading, writing, and arithmetic. They were expected to marry, although another option was to enter a convent and become a nun. Upper-class wives were expected to take over the household finances and estate management during times when their husbands were away. Although noble families had servants to perform household chores, noblewomen supervised their work.

Women were responsible for many household tasks, such as spinning yarn for clothes.

Women of the middle class often worked alongside their husbands in the family business. In peasant families, the wife had sole responsibility for all household tasks—cooking, cleaning, sewing, and child raising. In addition, wives helped their husbands in the field, planting and harvesting crops.

In medieval Islamic society, families were of key importance, seen as a way to preserve and enlarge the Muslim community. The husband was the head of an Islamic household, and his wife was expected to respect and obey him. Muslim wives took care of the household tasks and the children. Muslim husbands provided for the needs of their families.

Family life was also important to Jews of the Middle Ages. Jewish women were expected to marry and have children. Mothers taught their daughters the practical skills they needed to run a household. A Jewish husband and wife often signed a marriage contract, which recognized their shared rights and responsibilities. (See also *Clare of Assisi; Family and Household; Islam; Heloise and Abelard; Joan of Arc; Matilda of Tuscany; Monks, Friars, and Nuns.*)

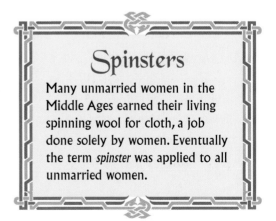

Spinsters

Many unmarried women in the Middle Ages earned their living spinning wool for cloth, a job done solely by women. Eventually the term *spinster* was applied to all unmarried women.

Glossary

annul to cancel

artisan person who is highly skilled in a craft

astronomer person who studies the stars, planets, and other heavenly bodies

astronomy study of the stars, planets, and other heavenly bodies

authenticate to prove to be real or genuine

bacteria tiny organisms that cause diseases

cacao bean from which chocolate is made

caravan group of merchants or pilgrims traveling together for safety

chivalry rules and traditions of medieval knighthood

city-state independent state consisting of a city and the surrounding territory

conquistadors Spanish conquerors of lands in the Americas in the 1500s

crucify to kill by nailing or binding a person's hands and feet to a cross

deacon church official who assists a priest

devout deeply religious

diplomacy skill at managing relations between rivals

dowry money or other valuables that a woman brings to her husband when they marry

dynasty series of rulers from the same family or group

excommunicate to exclude from membership in the Christian Church

exile banishment from one's country or home

famine extreme shortage of food

fief land provided by a lord to a vassal in return for service

gospel account of the life and teachings of Jesus as written in the first four books of the *New Testament*

heresy belief that differs from what is generally accepted as right or true

heretic person whose beliefs differ from what is commonly accepted as true

hygiene healthy practices, such as cleaniness

hymn song praising God

logic principles of reasoning

metaphysics study of the nature and meaning of reality

mint to make coins; or a place where coins are made

missionary person who works to convert nonbelievers to Christianity

Moors Arab conquerors of Spain

mosque place of worship for Muslims

movable type wooden or metal blocks with raised letters that can be arranged to form words; used in printing

mural work of art created on a wall or ceiling

nomadic referring to people (nomads) who move from place to place to find food and grazing land

pagan nonbeliever; or person who believes in more than one god

parchment writing material made from the skin of a sheep or goat

philosopher scholar concerned with the study of ideas

philosophy study of ideas

pillage to steal the wealth of a conquered city or people

printing press machine that uses movable type (wooden or metal blocks with raised letters) to produce copies of a text

prophet person who is believed to have been chosen by God to deliver instructions or commands

quill large, stiff feather that is used as a pen

reed tall, thin grass with a jointed stem

Renaissance time of renewed interest in ancient Greek and Roman art and learning; began in Italy in the late 1300s

scribe person who copies manuscripts by hand

secular nonreligious; connected with everyday life

sermon speech given by a religious leader during a worship service, often about conduct or duty

shrine place that is considered holy because it contains sacred objects, such as the bones of a saint

siege to surround a city or fortress, cutting it off from aid and supplies

sultan ruler of a Muslim state

technology use of scientific knowledge for practical purposes

theologian person who studies religious beliefs and practices

theology study of the nature of God; or a system of religious beliefs

vassal person who serves a lord in return for land and protection

vizier chief minister of a Muslim state

Suggested Readings

Corbin, Carole Lynn. *Knights*. Danbury, Conn.: Franklin Watts, 1989.

Corbishley, Mike. *The Middle Ages*. New York: Facts on File, 1990.

Gregory, Tony. *The Dark Ages*. New York: Facts on File, 1993.

Howarth, Sarah. *The Middle Ages*. (See Through History Series). New York: Viking, 1993.

Langley, Andrew. *Medieval Life*. New York: Alfred A. Knopf, 1996.

Macdonald, Fiona. *A Medieval Castle*. New York: Peter Bedrick Books, 1990.

———. *How Would You Survive in the Middle Ages?* Danbury, Conn.: Franklin Watts, 1995.

———. *The Middle Ages*. New York: Facts on File, 1993.

Malaquais, Dominique. *The Kingdom of Benin*. Danbury, Conn.: Franklin Watts, 1998.

Mason, Anthony. *Medieval Times*. (If You Were There Series). New York: Simon & Schuster Books for Young Readers, 1996.

McGowen, Tom. *The Black Death*. Danbury, Conn.: Franklin Watts, 1995.

Nicolle, David. *Medieval Knights*. (See Through History Series). New York: Viking, 1997.

O'Neill, Richard. *The Middle Ages*. New York: Crescent Books, 1992.

Rice, Earle, Jr. *Life During the Crusades*. San Diego: Lucent Books, 1998.

Thompson, Carol. *The Empire of Mali*. Danbury, Conn.: Franklin Watts, 1998.

Index

111

Credits and Acknowledgments

Illustrations
Anna Kang: cover, 6, 15, 19, 26, 28, 38, 82, 96–97, 98–99
Elizabeth Herr: 9, 23, 35, 49, 61, 68, 76, 94, 104–105

Photos
7: Scala/Art Resource, NY; 8: Scala/Art Resource, NY;
10: Cameraphoto/Art Resource, NY; 11: Art Resource, NY; 13: Victoria & Albert Museum, London/Art Resource, NY; 17: Scala/Art Resource, NY; 21: Scala/Art Resource, NY; 25: Giraudon/Art Resource, NY; 27: Giraudon/Art Resource, NY; 29: Giraudon/Art Resource, NY; 31: Scala/Art Resource, NY; 32: Scala/Art Resource, NY; 33: Erich Lessing/Art Resource, NY; 37: The Pierpont Morgan Library/Art Resource, NY; 39: Scala/Art Resource, NY; 40: Scala/Art Resource, NY; 41: Art Resource, NY; 42: Giraudon/Art Resource, NY; 43: Erich Lessing/Art Resource, NY; 44: Scala/Art Resource, NY; 46: Scala/Art Resource, NY; 47: Erich Lessing/Art Resource, NY; 48: Nick Saunders/Barbara Heller Photo Library, London/Art Resource, NY;
51: Erich Lessing/Art Resource, NY; 52: Scala/Art Resource, NY; 53: Art Resource, NY; 54: Giraudon/Art Resource, NY; 55: Giraudon/Art Resource, NY; 57: Giraudon/Art Resource, NY; 58: Scala/Art Resource, NY; 63: The Granger Collection, New York; 65: The Granger Collection, New York; 66: D. Y./Art Resource, NY; 69: Erich Lessing/Art Resource, NY; 71: Werner Forman/Art Resource, NY; 72: Giraudon/Art Resource, NY; 73: The Granger Collection, New York; 75: Giraudon/Art Resource, NY; 78: Erich Lessing/Art Resource, NY; 80: Scala/Art Resource, NY; 81: The Granger Collection, New York; 83: Art Resource, NY; 84: Giraudon/Art Resource, NY; 85: Scala/Art Resource, NY; 86: SEF/Art Resource, NY; 87: Giraudon/Art Resource, NY; 89: Giraudon/Art Resource, NY; 91: Giraudon/Art Resource, NY; 92: Giraudon/Art Resource, NY; 93: Art Resource, NY; 100: Scala/Art Resource, NY; 102: Giraudon/Art Resource, NY; 106: Giraudon/Art Resource, NY; 107: Giraudon/Art Resource, NY